RESERVATIONS REQUIRED...

Reservations Required

Culinary Secrets of
Las Vegas'
Celebrity Chefs

Sarah Lee Marks

HUNTINGTON PRESS

LAS VEGAS, NEVADA

Reservations Required
Culinary Secrets of Las Vegas' Celebrity Chefs

Published by
Huntington Press
3687 S. Procyon Ave.
Las Vegas, NV 89103
Phone (702) 252-0655
e-mail: books@huntingtonpress.com

ISBN: 0-929712-19-6

Cover Design: Dempsey Graphics
Interior Design: Bethany Coffey
Production: Laurie Shaw

All photos by Audrey Dempsey except:
Photo on page 3 by Palms PR staff
Photo on page 86 by John Ormond
Photos on pages 87, 89, and 91 by Ogara Bissell
Photos on pages 92, 93, and 95 by Gregory Ross

Printed in Korea

Contents

Dedication

This book is dedicated to
My loving family: Norman, Rebecca, and Lola.
My dad Ernest M. Lander: who loved great food.
And my mom Barbara Lander: who bought me
my first cookbook, Weight Watchers Vol. I.

Acknowledgments

I'd like to extend my deepest heart-felt thanks to Audrey Dempsey of Infinity Photo, who I believe is the greatest food photographer in the world, and is a good friend as well. (NMRK)

Chef Elizabeth Hoiles-Menzel is not only a master food editor, personal chef, and champion of patience, but her culinary bona fides are among the most impressive in Las Vegas. She graduated from the New England Culinary Institute and has spent more than 25 years refining her professional experience. Her resumé includes some of the country's top restaurants and private country clubs, including Abercrombie and Kent Destination Clubs, Las Vegas' exclusive Shadow Creek Golf Course, and André's French Restaurant, also in Vegas. As a personal chef, her food is healthy, creative, and satisfies both the traditionalist and the culinary adventurer. She and her husband Michael live in Las Vegas.

K.T. Anders is my source of inspiration and purveyor of eternal hope.

Finally, *Reservations Required* couldn't have happened without Bethany Coffey and Anthony Curtis of Huntington Press, who gave me the opportunity to bring this idea to fruition.

Introduction

Back when dining on the Strip meant little more than cheap buffets, expensive coffee shops, fancy Italian ristorantes, and so-called gourmet rooms, André Rochat arrived in Las Vegas from Lyon, France, via Boston in 1973 with empty pockets and a bag full of kitchen knives. The earliest pioneer of fine food in southern Nevada, Rochat set up shop in 1980 in a downtown bungalow, where he introduced classic French cuisine to an enthusiastic response.

In 1985, the Ferraro family turned Mama Ferraro's secret recipes into a dining landmark, mostly for locals, west of the Strip.

Gustav Mauler also saw the future of fine dining in Las Vegas. In 1987, he began work at the Golden Nugget as Senior Vice President of Mirage Resorts in charge of the development of the myriad of restaurants and food products for the Mirage, as well as the Mirage Resorts hotel-casinos to come.

In 1992 Wolfgang Puck unleashed the floodwaters when he opened Spago in the Forum Shops at Caesars. Nationally renowned restaurants and celebrity chefs rode in on the wave. For example, a year later, Emeril "BAM!" Lagasse was coaxed west from New Orleans with a prime location in the new 5,005-room MGM Grand. Later, Steve Wynn lured Julian Serrano to Bellagio from San Francisco's famed Masa's by promising to create Picasso, the most exquisite dining room in the world, adorned by $30 million of the master's artwork.

Since then, Charlie Palmer, Mark Miller, Joachim Splichal, Bradley Ogden, and dozens more world-class chefs opened high-concept-and-cuisine restaurants in the most expensive hotels ever built on Earth.

With so many fine restaurants in one small city—in fact, along one four-mile stretch of Strip—how do you pick one for your own perfect dining experience? You can read reviews in the local newspapers, peruse guidebooks, or solicit recommendations from friends. But best is to experience the personality of the restaurant, along with its priorities and personnel. And the only way to do that is by meeting and getting to know the executive chef.

It's the kitchen boss who, by overseeing ingredients, preparation, presentation, service, ambience, and nuance, ensures that the ultimate dining experience—the synchronization of sight, smell, taste, and feel—comes together in perfect harmony. Who are the executive chefs that make this moment a reality, meal after meal, night after night, year after year? Masters at what they do, the best have been catapulted to the highest reaches of celebrity chefdom. But whether they're Emeril Lagasse or Honorio Mecinas, whether they star in their own television show or prefer the back of the house to the limelight, their histories give you a glimpse into the level of perfection they live to attain.

The stories are frequently inspiring: Born to immigrants from foreign lands, children of farmers, cooks, restaurateurs, or bankers, the passion for creating outstanding gastronomic experiences has often been with them all their lives. Furthermore, these toque-clad artists also inspire their kitchenmates; it's the job of a great chef to mentor those around them, just as they were mentored by great chefs in their turn. Best of all, they're all approachable and rarely fail to take a few minutes out of their day to greet their dinner guests.

I was especially fortunate venturing into their kitchens—book contract, reporter's notebook, and food photographer in tow. I spent countless pleasurable hours observing and taking notes as their favorite dishes came to life. At the same time, I became conscious of the skill level each recipe requires, resulting in the Challenge Ratings that appear in the Appendix in the back of the book. Later, food editor Elizabeth Hoiles-Menzel made sure that the recipes and notes I gathered were simple to understand and easy to follow. In addition, food-photographer extraordinaire Audrey Dempsey created a visual catalog to guide you along the way.

The real fun began when we tested the recipes. Chef John LaGrone of Postrio at the Venetian displayed great patience while demonstrating the correct procedure for wrapping the parchment paper over his Postrio Salmon en Papillote. In my kitchen, I had a stapler ready just in case, but it wasn't necessary.

While James Benson of Osterio del Circo at Bellagio was preparing his loin of rabbit, it had been deboned. As I watched him fitting back together all the pieces of the rabbit puzzle, he explained that since he hates waste, it's important to use every edible part. I kept wondering if it's lucky to eat the rabbit's foot.

Dinner for eight at the last minute? Go for the sweet shrimp salad by Chef Tom Moloney of AquaKnox at the Venetian. Fun, fast, and easy, it looks like a million bucks and will fill up the entire group. The hardest part? Cutting up the seedless watermelon. And be sure not to use zebra black-striped shrimp; the black looks yucky in the salad!

My rendition of breast of chicken involtini from Chef Gustav Mauler, now in the kitchen of Spiedini at JW Marriott at Rampart, is a family affair. My daughter, my husband, sometimes even my dog get into the act when it's time to pound, stuff, and bread the chicken. The finished plate looks a lot harder to make than it is, even with a kid and a man helping!

Did I mention how I wowed my friends with Ortanique's Chef Cindy Hutson's venison and jerk recipes? I did it by taking everyone out to her fabulous restaurant in Paris Las Vegas and surprising them with orders of both. My compatriots in cuisine had a blast trying to guess all the ingredients, and you'll be as surprised as they were when you delve into the extraordinary blend of seasonings and sauces that make these dishes unique. We purposefully rounded out the selection of recipes to allow the use of the freshest produce and products available in season.

Every chef emphasized personal creativity. If you don't like a certain fish, feel free to substitute. Not enamored with a particular spice? Change or delete it. If you can't find an ingredient at your neighborhood grocery, ask the manager at your local gourmet or natural-food market.

When I'm too tired to cook great meals, I do the next best thing and make great reservations. That's where the photographs in *Reservations Required* are especially inspiring. Each shot is designed to capture something that's unique to the particular restaurant. Look closely at these dazzling images and you'll see Vegas in every one of them. Feel the magic as you turn the pages, prepare your favorite dish, or actually take a seat in one of these magnificent settings.

This book exemplifies Las Vegas, a place that fosters new and exciting experiences. The award-winning chefs featured here represent the culinary elite in a city where showmanship is choreographed to the nth degree. As you savor the profiles, feast your eyes on the photography, and contemplate the recipes, you'll be transported to the Strip in all its glory. *Reservations Required* is your passport to the restaurants, chefs, meals, and memories of the world's new culinary star. Use this book as a treasure map to the city's best restaurants and don't be shy about asking for the chef's autograph when you visit in person for a great memento of your adventures in Las Vegas fine dining.

Bon appetit!

André Rochat
Jacques Van Staden

"Passion," says André Rochat, Alizé's chef and owner, "is what drives a real chef."

"So if you are interested in money," adds Jacques Van Staden, his chef de cuisine, "this is not the business to be in."

Although a generation apart, both men share that passion for cooking, and it guides their lives. Now they share a kitchen that is wowing the culinary elite with its "lighter-than-traditional" French food. In 2004, *Las Vegas* magazine bestowed its top honor, the Epicurean Award, on Alizé at the Palms.

Both chefs began as ambitious immigrants to the United States. Rochat's passion has led him from his birthplace in the Savoie region of the French Alps to the ownership of three award-winning restaurants in Las Vegas. In fact, he's been called the culinary pioneer of Las Vegas, since he opened his first French restaurant, eponymously named André's, downtown more than 25 years ago; it was the first classic French restaurant in town. It's still earning rave reviews.

Raised in the family *charcuterie*, Rochat knew early that food would be the centerpiece in his life. At 14 he eagerly left home to apprentice at Leon de Lyon, a Michelin two-star restaurant in Lyon, France. When he came to the United States in 1965, armed with his kitchen knives and dreams of owning his own restaurant, he began his New World training in prestigious East Coast restaurants. "It takes ten years or more to become a real chef," he says. "Nothing replaces hard work, sweat, and practice. A true chef can do everything in the kitchen—you must learn every station, technique, and food product before you can call yourself a chef."

If the love of his life is the kitchen, he is eager to pass on that passion to others. In his office he keeps an entire library of cookbooks to help his young protégés learn on the job.

Jacques Van Staden, too, showed an early culinary passion when he began doing part-time restaurant work while attending high school in his native South Africa. But it wasn't until he arrived in the U.S. in 1990 that he got his first professional cooking job at the South African Embassy in Washington D.C.

His talent was soon recognized and he worked under several famous chefs in various renowned restaurants. He became the youngest chef at the Watergate Hotel and along the way he was nominated for the James Beard "Young Rising Chef" Award.

After owning two restaurants in Washington, Jacques moved to Las Vegas, where he attracted a following at various restaurants and caught the attention of Rochat. The partnership has resulted in the extraordinary Alizé.

Alizé was named for the tradewinds that caress the Caribbean islands, and if you're a romantic, you may feel a hint of them in the warm desert winds in Las Vegas. When you dine at Alizé, you are up there—literally way, way up there—on the 56th floor of the soaring Palms Resort. Dramatic floor-to-ceiling glass opens the room to the dazzling neon of the Vegas Strip spread below and the lonely desert mountains in the distance. Rich woods, candlelight, and fresh flowers accent the burgundy and gold décor. In the center of the U-shaped dining room is André's pride—a two-story glass wine room that houses 6,000 bottles of wine, including a collection of vintage cognacs and liqueurs boasting dates from 1777.

Duo of Colorado Lamb Shank

with toasted double lamb chops
parsnip purée, Cèpe mushrooms, sun-dried tomatoes, and lamb jus

Serves 6

Lamb shank

2 10-oz.	lamb shanks
1 large	onion, diced
2 large	carrots, diced
2 stalks	celery, diced
2 bulbs	garlic, cut in half
2 sprigs	rosemary
3 sprigs	thyme
4 whole	bay leaves
2 diced	Roma tomatoes
1/2 cup	soy sauce
2 cups	white wine
2 quarts	water
salt and pepper	

Lamb shank pastries

2 large	onions, peeled and sliced
2 tsp.	ground cinnamon
1/2 tsp.	cayenne pepper
salt	
6 sheets	Fuille de Brick dough

Finishing lamb jus

4 cups	braising liquid
4 tbsp.	butter
4 sprigs	marjoram
1/2 tsp.	lemon juice

Parsnip purée

1 lb.	parsnips, peeled & diced
1/2 quart	heavy cream
salt and white pepper	

Cèpe mushrooms
(the Cèpes are usually large mushrooms)

1 lb.	Cèpe mushrooms, clean & trimmed
1/2 small	onion, diced
4 tbsp.	corn oil
2 sprigs	thyme
salt and pepper to taste	

Garnish

1 cup	pearl onions, peeled
1/2 cup	sun-dried tomatoes
1 cup	garlic confit
1 cup	pea shoots

Lamb chop

2 racks of lamb, 6 ribs each	
1/2 cup	whole-grain mustard
1/4 cup	chives, chopped
1/4 cup	parsley, chopped
salt and black pepper	

For the lamb shank:
• Season the lamb shanks with salt and pepper, then sear with corn oil in medium-hot pan until dark brown on all sides.
• Place the lamb shanks in a small pot, deglaze the pan they were seared in with white wine, and pour over the browned shanks.
• Sauté the vegetables to a golden-brown color and add to the lamb shanks.
• Add the remaining ingredients and bring to a boil. Turn the heat to low and simmer the shanks for two hours, until very tender.
• Remove the shanks from the braising liquid and pull meat from the bone. Shred the meat into small pieces and set aside.
• Strain the braising liquid into another pot and set aside until needed for the jus.

For the lamb pastries:
• Sauté the sliced onions over medium heat with corn oil until golden brown. Mix the caramelized onions with the shredded lamb and seasonings until well incorporated.
• Spread the lamb mixture evenly into a square 8" x 8" container and chill it in the refrigerator.
• Once the lamb mixture is cold, cut into six equal pieces.
• Wrap each piece of the lamb mixture in a sheet of the Fuille de Brick dough and brush the ends with eggwash to seal it into a package. Repeat with the remaining lamb mixture and sheets of dough.
• Refrigerate the packages until you are ready to complete the entrée.

For lamb jus:
• Heat the braising liquid with the butter and reduce it by half, until it is slightly thickened.
• Once the desired consistency has been reached, add the rest of the ingredients, stir, and season with salt and pepper to taste. Set aside until you are ready to complete the entrée.

For the parsnip purée:
• Place the parsnips in a pot, cover with the cream, and cook until very tender.
• Purée the parsnips and cream in a blender using a rubber spatula to help along, until the purée is smooth. Season with salt and pepper, then set aside.

For the Cèpe mushrooms:
• Cut the mushrooms into large cubes. Sauté the mushrooms in corn oil until browned. Add the shallots, herbs, seasonings, and toss.
• Remove from heat and set aside.

For the garnish:
• Slowly caramelize the pearl onions until golden brown in a sauté pan with butter, chicken stock, and salt and pepper.
• Julienne the sun-dried tomatoes.
• Wash, dry, and trim the pea shoots.

DIFFICULTY LEVEL: 5

Chefs André Rochat and Jacques Van Staden © 2005 Alizé

For the lamb chops:

• Cut each lamb rack into three two-rib portions. Trim any excess fat from the racks, remove the fat from between the rib bones, and scrape the bones clean.

• Season lamb with salt and pepper and brown in a hot sauté pan to medium rare, about 7 minutes. Remove the two-rib chops from the pan and let rest for one minute.

• Before serving, brush the back of the chops with Dijon mustard and dip in the chives and parsley.

To complete:

• Sauté the lamb-shank pastries over low heat until browned on each side. Place the pastries in a hot oven to crisp and heat throughout. Once the pastries are hot and crisp, remove from the oven and trim the ends.

• Place parsnip purée in center of a bowl and spoon the mushrooms, caramelized pearl onions, garlic confit, and sun-dried tomatoes around.

• Arrange the pastries on top of the parsnip purée.

• Cut each two-rib chop in half and display by leaning it against the crisp pastry.

• Drizzle the hot jus over the lamb and vegetables.

• Garnish with the pea shoots and serve.

Chef's tips:

• Make sure when braising the lamb shank to cook it until very tender. When pulling the meat from the bone and preparing to roll, make sure to drain properly from liquid. For the parsnip purée, you will have to use a rubber spatula to help the purée along or it will just sit in the blender.

Author's comments:

• The order of this recipe is designed to allow you to prepare all the ingredients, except the lamb chops, ahead of time.

Wine pairing:

• Cain Cellars, Cain Cuvee, St. Helena, Napa

Sautéed Muscovy Duck Breast

with duck croustilliant, wild-rice pancake, sautéed spinach, onions, and cranberry-ginger sauce

Serves 6

Duck

3 whole	Muscovy ducks

Duck confit

6 each	duck legs, from the whole ducks
2 lb.	duck fat
1	orange, zest only
1 large	shallot, chopped
2 sprigs	thyme, whole
1	cinnamon stick
6 tbsp.	kosher salt
2 tbsp.	ground black pepper

Duck croustilliant

	duck confit finished product
1 medium	onion, diced
4 tbsp.	mild curry powder
1/2 cup	dried cranberries, chopped
1/2 cup	duck fat
6 large	springroll wrappers

Duck jus (for sauce)

1 large	white onion
1 bulb	garlic
1 large	carrot, peeled
2 sprigs	thyme, whole
2 cups	tomato, rough dice
1 stalk	celery, diced
4 cups	Chardonnay
2 quarts	water
1/2 cup	flour

Cranberry-ginger sauce

2 quarts	duck jus, strained
2 tbsp.	ginger, chopped
3 cups	red wine
5 tbsp.	balsamic vinegar
2 tbsp.	soy sauce
1 cup	ruby red port wine
1 tsp.	black pepper
1/2 cup	cranberries, whole

For the duck:
- Remove the whole duck from the package, discard the blood, and pat dry. Remove the neck, gizzards, and liver and set aside for the jus.
- Cut the leg and thigh quarters from the duck and set aside. Cut through the back of the duck to remove the breast with the ribs. Remove the wing tips. Reserve the bones and trimmings of the duck to use for the duck jus.
- Season the duck breasts with salt and pepper and slowly sear in a hot pan with a little oil until breasts are golden brown. Remove from pan and cut the breasts from the rib cage. Set the breasts aside to be finished later. Reserve the ribs to make the duck jus.

For the duck confit:
- Place the duck legs with the remaining ingredients in a small pot with the duck fat and bring to a boil. Cover and place the pot in a preheated 350° oven for two hours.
- Remove the pot from the oven when the meat has pulled away from the knuckle of the duck bone. Remove the legs from the hot fat and let cool long enough to handle.
- Strain the fat and reserve for later usage.

For the croustilliant:
- Remove the meat from the duck legs while still warm and place in a mixing bowl with a paddle.
- Sweat the onions over low heat with the duck fat and curry until translucent. Remove the pan from the heat.
- Add the onion mixture and the cranberries to the shredded duck meat and mix until well incorporated.
- Divide the mixture into six equal portions. Place each portion on one end of the wrapper and fold into a cigar shape. Brush the ends of the wrapper with some egg-wash to ensure that it seals properly.

For the duck jus:
- In a preheated 375° oven, brown the duck bones and trimmings.
- In a stockpot, brown the vegetables with the duck fat. Add the flour and stir until it turns a golden brown color.
- Add the browned bones to the stockpot along with the wine. Reduce by half, and add the water. Simmer for 1 hour.
- Remove and strain the duck jus through a fine strainer or a chinoise, then set aside.

For the ginger-cranberry sauce:
- Place all the ingredients, except the cranberries, in a saucepan on low-medium heat. Be careful not to boil. Reduce to a syrup consistency.
- Add the cranberries, then taste and adjust the salt and pepper.

DIFFICULTY LEVEL: 5

Chefs André Rochat and Jacques Van Staden © 2005 Alizé

Wild-rice pancakes

1-1/2 cups	wild rice, cooked
2 whole	eggs
2 cups	buckwheat pancake mix
2 cups	milk
4 tbsp.	chives, chopped
1 tsp.	ground cumin

Vegetables

1/2 lb.	spinach, cleaned
4 tbsp.	butter
1 clove	garlic, minced
1 cup	pearl onions, caramelized
salt and pepper	

Garnish

1 pinch	chervil, picked
1 bunch	micro green salad
(www.bestmicrogreens.com)	
1 tsp.	basil oil

For the wild-rice pancakes:

- Finely chop half of the wild rice in a food processor.
- Combine the chopped and whole rice with the rest of the ingredients in a mixing bowl. Stir until just incorporated.
- Place spoonfuls of the batter in a non-stick pan brushed with some oil. Cook on both sides until lightly brown.

For the vegetables:

- Sauté spinach and pearl onions in a hot pan with the rest of the ingredients until the spinach is wilted.

To complete:

- Fry the croustilliant "cigars" in 370° oil until crispy and browned. Drain on paper towels.
- Place the duck breasts in a medium-hot pan, skin side down, and cook for 4 minutes. Turn over and cook for 2 minutes. Place in a hot oven for 3 minutes, remove and let rest for 1 minute. The duck breast should be medium-rare. Cook the duck breast longer if medium to well temperature is desired.
- Place the pancakes to the side of an oval/rectangular plate and place the sautéed spinach with pearl onions beside.
- Slice the duck breast across, not lengthwise, and fan it over the pancakes. Place the piece with the wing standing up straight.
- The croustilliant "cigar" is placed at an angle over the sliced duck breast. Pour a small amount of the ginger-cranberry sauce around the duck and the croustilliant, not over it.
- Place the micro greens and chervil on top and drizzle with the basil oil.

Wine pairing:

- Gigondas, Chateau de Sainte Cosme

Tom Moloney

The challenge: to present enticing seafood with just-snatched-from-the-ocean freshness to diners encircled by hundreds of miles of parched desert sands. Chef Tom Moloney is up to the job. His talent transforms treasures from the sea, flown in fresh daily from all over the globe, into sophisticated dishes that retain their simplicity, yet offer tantalizing tastes. Favorites: seared day-boat scallops with parsnip purée and warm citrus juices; sautéed John Dory with lobster succotash and sweet corn broth; delectable oyster shooters, served in a shot glass and doused in sake, ponzu, and citrus juices, with a dash of Tabasco. This is seafood with style.

"My method of cooking is the most basic, and also the most difficult," says Moloney. "Only by preparing dishes with the freshest ingredients, the highest-quality products, and in the most direct manner of cooking can you truly create a meal that is an experience, where the true essence of the food connects to the guest." No heavy butters for this chef. "I love all types of fish seasoned with light sauces and vinaigrettes," he says. "I also like to use interesting spices and wine."

Moloney's art is a product of experience, not the culinary-school kitchen. "I learned on the job," he says. "I worked every position in restaurant kitchens. I moved to different restaurants and tried cooking different cuisines."

But it wasn't until he met Wolfgang Puck that he discovered a love for seafood. "I love raising the expectation of the guest from the basic steak and lobster to an unusual combination of an in-season fish and meat prepared in a colorful and artistic fashion," he says. During his 12 years with the Puck organization, Moloney opened seven restaurants for the celebrity chef. He then moved on to become a restaurant consultant, overseeing kitchen operations and helping well-known restaurant groups develop menu ideas.

But the kitchen is where his heart is. In the polished stainless-steel open kitchen at AquaKnox at the Venetian, guests can watch Moloney wield sauté pans with the finesse of an orchestra maestro as he creates his masterpieces from the deep. His small staff hums along, shoulder to shoulder, putting out hundreds of plates a night in flawless execution. "I genuinely enjoy being here in the kitchen," he says. "I am very hands-on. I can't think of anything I like better than working on the line, creating new recipes and interesting presentations."

Of course, if you're going to become famous for serving seafood when there's nothing but sand in sight, you've got to put diners in the right mood. Stepping into AquaKnox is a sensual journey into the world of water. Cool blue light, subtly changing to sea green, drenches the room, catching a flash of chrome accents throughout the restaurant and at the raw bar. Past the cascading water logo at the entrance stands the circular wine room, encased in a glass vault, water streaming down its sides. Walls of silently cascading water create various partitions between cozy circular booths. A private dining room feels like a stateroom aboard a yacht. Images of manrays and sea urchins à la *National Geographic* float across large flat screens, synchronized to the music of Manheim Steamroller.

"To take the dining experience to a new level, there must be an interesting and entertaining environment," says Moloney. "The chef pulls it all together. I enjoy creating that synergy and watching it translate on the faces of the guests."

Sweet Shrimp Salad

Serves 4

Salad dressing

1 cup	orange juice
1 cup	lemon juice
1 cup	lime juice
3/4 cup	sugar
1-1/2 tsp.	Dijon mustard
2 tbsp.	honey
1/4 cup	Champagne vinegar
1 cup	peanut oil
salt and white pepper	

Salad

1 cup	shrimp: cooked, peeled, and devined, small
1/3 cup	goat cheese
8 oz.	frisee (substitute chickory, curly endive)
1 cup	romaine lettuce (chopped)
3/4 cup	watermelon (seedless and cut into 1/2" squares)
1 bunch	fresh mixed herbs (chives, mint leaves, basil)
6 tbsp.	salad dressing

For the salad dressing:
- Simmer juices and sugar in a small saucepan until reduced by two-thirds.
- Taste as reducing for your desired sweetness. Let reduction cool and set aside. You will have more reduction than needed for this recipe; it keeps well if refrigerated.
- In a mixing bowl, combine half of the juice reduction, Dijon mustard, honey, and Champagne vinegar. Whisk until smooth.
- Whisking vigorously, add peanut oil slowly to emulsify.
- Finish with salt and white pepper to taste.

To complete the salad:
- In a bowl, toss shrimp and salad ingredients with dressing.
- Arrange and serve on chilled plates.
- Sprinkle with salt and pepper to taste.

Wine pairing:
- Nobilo Sauvignon Blanc, New Zealand
  Grassy, bright, tropical fruit, crisp, and very clean.

Seared Day Boat Scallops

with parsnip purée and citrus jus

Serves 4

Parsnip purée

2 lbs.	parsnips
1 lb.	Idaho potatoes
1 cup	cream
1/4 cup	butter, unsalted

salt and white pepper

Citrus jus

2 large	oranges
1 medium	lemon
1 pinch	chives
1 tbsp.	butter, unsalted, melted

salt and white pepper

U-10 scallops

16 huge	scallops, size U-10 (4 per person)

olive oil
salt and white pepper

For the parsnip purée:
• Peel and cut the parsnips and potatoes into 1" dice.
• Place vegetables in an 8-quart pot, cover with water, and bring to a boil. Reduce heat to medium and simmer until tender, roughly 30-35 minutes. Drain the vegetables in a colander and place back into the hot pot.
• Warm the cream and butter in a small saucepan and bring it just to a simmer.
• Using a potato ricer or a hand mixer, mash the vegetables. Stir in the hot cream.
• Taste and add salt and pepper as desired.

For the citrus jus:
• Place the strained citrus juices in a small saucepan and bring to a boil. Lower heat and simmer until reduced by 25%.
• Whisk in the melted butter and chives. Taste and season with the salt and pepper.

For the scallops:
• Pat the scallops dry and lightly season on both sides with salt and pepper.
• Heat the olive oil in a sauté pan and sear the scallops until medium rare to medium and golden brown, 2-3 minutes each side.

To complete:
• Divide the parsnip purée onto the center of four warm plates.
• Arrange four scallops on each plate around the parsnip purée. Pour the citrus jus around the purée and garnish with the chopped chives.

Wine pairing:
• Brundlemeyer Alte Reben Gruner Velt Liner
This white wine is flinty, with high acidity and flavors of grapefruit, melon, and dill.

Philippe Rispoli

Progressive American cuisine is the signature of restaurateur Charlie Palmer, whose Aureole restaurant in New York is famous among the elite. Though American, it also has a French flair that Executive Chef Philippe Rispoli perfectly interprets in the Las Vegas version of Aureole with a "let the food speak for itself" philosophy. "True French cuisine is simple, from nature, and in as natural a form as possible to allow for the flavor of the food to come out," he says.

He ought to know. This native Frenchman left home at 14 to train at culinary school in Lyon, France, and got his hands-on training in the kitchens of several Michelin restaurants in France. "But my real education as a chef came from working with the best chefs in the world—Paul Bocuse, Georges Blanc, and Charlie Palmer," says Rispoli. "I use few ingredients and everything is one hundred percent natural and very fresh. The beauty of fine food is that it's not complicated—not too much stuff or fussing. I don't pile things all over the plate."

Clearly, Rispoli is master of his domain with a keen eye for detail during the meticulous preparation of his dishes. Meat, lobster, and chicken stocks are made fresh every day. Fish is flown in daily. Rispoli oversees it all. "I work twelve to sixteen hours a day, overseeing everything from the line to the presentation," he says. "The demand on the chef is to be perfect and precise three hundred times a night. I am fortunate that I have a very good team."

Being a chef in the United States requires a different approach from cooking in Europe, according to Rispoli. "In Europe, it's all about the food," he explains. "In the U.S., there is much competition. It's about the ability to meet very high expectations. It's very high pressure. The guest wants a total dining experience and we prepare a wonderful dish, but the room, the staff, the wine, and the mood must all blend together perfectly to make sure the diner is totally satisfied."

Aureole at Mandalay Bay has translated that dining mandate into a bit of pure theater. At the entrance to the restaurant, a bridge brings you to a staircase that winds around a 42-foot-high glass-enclosed tower with a glowing core. No, it's not a rocket. It's a temperature- and humidity-controlled wine cellar with translucent bins that stores nearly 10,000 bottles of wine. "Wine angels" in black cat suits and helmets use cables to rappel themselves up and down the sides of the seven levels to retrieve bottles as ordered. If you're imagining Tom Cruise in the movie *Mission Impossible*, you're not far off—that was the inspiration.

For dining with a background a little less dramatic, there's the intimate Swan Court, a room in the rear with a wall of windows from which you can contemplate the swans lounging elegantly in the outdoor pond.

But although the drama of the wine may take center stage, the food is never lost. Rispoli changes the menu seasonally and his secret is in finding new and enticing flavors to blend. "I get excited about trying new things with lots of color on the plate and with fresh beautiful ingredients," he says. "I find inspiration when I look at the flowers blooming, the beauty of the scenery, the paintings on the walls, and the produce in the market."

Spring Vegetable Medley with Sautéed Snapper

zucchini and squash ribbons, wild mushrooms, and vegetable medley

Serves 4

Zucchini and squash ribbons

2 medium	zucchini
2 medium	yellow squash
3 cups	assorted wild mushrooms, cleaned and cut in half
8 small	carrots, peeled
2 cups	haricot vert, blanched and shocked
12	broccoli florets
10	asparagus tips
8	Roma tomatoes

Snapper

4 medium	snapper filets, skin on
10	chives, sliced julienne 2" long
1 large	Yukon Gold potato, shredded
	beef stock, reduced into thick sauce
	clarified butter
	olive oil

For the vegetables:
• Slice the zucchini and yellow squash lengthwise into thin strips using a mandoline, peeler, or slicer.
• Fill a large pot with water and bring to a boil.
• Blanch zucchini and yellow squash, then plunge into ice water to stop the cooking.
• Blanch and shock the haricot vert, snow peas, asparagus tips, and broccoli separately.
• In a hot sauté pan, briefly heat zucchini/squash ribbons in olive oil.
• Remove and pat off excess olive oil using a paper towel.
• In a hot sauté pan, sauté wild mushrooms in olive oil until just cooked.

For the potato gallete:
• Shred the potato using a box grater (approx. 1/4" diameter).
• Soak the grated potato in water. Drain potato and squeeze out excess water.
• Lightly toss with clarified butter.
• Place a silpat mat on a cooking sheet and make 4 thin rounds of shredded potato.
• Place another silpat mat and cooking sheet on top and bake in a 400° oven until crispy.

For the tomato confit:
• With a knife, make tiny insertions that just pierce the skin on the bottom of the Roma tomatoes.
• Drop tomatoes into boiling water for 60 seconds.
• Remove and plunge into ice water.
• Remove from water. Pull skin back and remove.
• Cut tomatoes in half lengthwise. Remove seeds.
• Place on cooking sheet and drizzle with olive oil, fresh herbs, and garlic cloves.
• Bake in a 200° oven for several hours until soft.
• Remove and place in a plastic container covered with olive oil until ready to use.

For the snapper:
• Flour snapper and season with salt and pepper to coat.
• In a very hot sauté pan, sauté snapper filets in olive oil until cooked.
• Add julienne chives and lightly coat with beef sauce.
• Cut each filet into three pieces.

Chef Philippe Rispoli © 2005 Aureole

To assemble:

- Assemble vegetables beginning with a bed of zucchini and squash ribbons placed in the center of a large plate. Top with carrot and mushroom mixture.
- Add snow peas, haricot vert, asparagus tips and broccoli, alternating with tomato confit pieces.
- Place a potato gallette on top of the vegetable mixture.
- Put a few vegetables on top of the gallette.
- Sprinkle plate with micro greens.
- Place snapper pieces around vegetables and lightly drizzle the sauce around the entrée.

Wine pairing:

- Greneche Blanc, Chardonay or Sauvignon Blanc
  www.wines-france.com

Lobster Salad

stuffed tomato with avocado and zucchini rosette

Serves 4

Lobster
4 large   lobster tails, cooked
(keep head for garnish)
1 large   zucchini
Micro greens
balsamic vinaigrette
cayenne pepper
tumeric

Stuffed vine-ripened tomatoes with avocado salad
4 large   vine-ripened tomatoes
2 large   avocados
1 tbsp.   chives, chopped
juice of lemon
salt and pepper to taste

Balsamic vinaigrette
1/4 cup   balsamic vinegar
3/4 cup   olive oil

For the stuffed tomatoes:
• Keep vine and leaves intact on tomato.
• Trim vine to a half-inch stem. With a knife make two tiny cuts that just pierce the skin on the bottom of the tomato.
• Insert tomatoes into boiling water for 30 seconds.
• Remove and plunge into ice water.
• Cut tomato just below lid and remove the tomato skin. Reserve some tomato skin for garnish and keep lid intact. Hollow out the tomato pulp and seeds. Turn tomato upside down to let cavity drain.

For the avocado salad:
• Peel and cut avocado into bite-size pieces. Add lemon juice, chives, and season to taste with salt and pepper.
• Fill the tomato with avocado salad.

For the curled tomato garnish:
• Put lid and tomato skin into hot oil for 10 seconds. Remove from oil. The skin will naturally curl up.

For the zucchini rosette:
• Slice the zucchini into very thin rounds.
• Fill a sauce pan with water and bring to boil.
• Blanch zucchini slices. Remove zucchini slices from pan and shock in ice water.
• Cut slices in half and toss lightly in olive oil and season with salt and pepper.
• Arrange the zucchini slices in 3" x 1/2" ring overlapping to make a rosette shape.

To complete the salad:
• Make the balsamic vinaigrette by whisking the balsamic vinegar and oil together.
• Place stuffed tomato on top of the zucchini rosette.
• Slice one half lobster tail into medallions and lightly coat with balsamic vinaigrette. Arrange the lobster on top of the stuffed tomato and place the tomato lid on top of the rosette.
• Place lobster head on a bed of micro greens next to zucchini rosette.
• Garnish plate with tomato-skin pieces.
• Drizzle entire salad and around plate with the balsamic vinaigrette.
• At the edge of the plate opposite lobster head, place a light dusting of cayenne pepper and tumeric.

Wine pairing:
• Pinot Gris

Luigi Bomparola

In the large open kitchen at Canaletto in the Venetian, Luigi Bomparola's instructions to his staff of 40 come out in a stream of Italian that sounds more like music than production orders. As he patiently teaches a julienne technique or a risotto trick, he receives broad smiles and nods of agreement when the desired effect is achieved. Then he steps back and lets the next in line try his hand. "I enjoy helping others learn," he says. "I teach by demonstrating, coaching, and promoting a positive can-do attitude. If my brother had not been patient with me, I would not be here today."

Bomparola and his older brother, Jerry, grew up poor in Milano, Italy. "Cooking was a way to learn a trade, eat well, and provide for my family," says Bomparola. "My brother is extremely creative, and he motivated me to work harder. I owe him a lot and look up to him."

Jerry Bomparola is chef of his own restaurant in Milan and has never been to Canaletto, but no doubt he'd be proud of his younger sibling. Luigi Bomparola's love for the kitchen is evident. "This is the only thing I have ever known," he says. "The atmosphere and the creativity keep me going. I love to mix the ingredients. I can never make the same thing exactly the same each time. Sometimes it's saffron, the next time pesto. The mystery and surprise are part of the experience."

Learning all he can about his ingredients is an ongoing project for Bomparola. He likes to be able to explain to guests what they're about to experience. For example, he cites saffron as one of his favorite spices. "Saffron is very expensive, because it takes 136,000 flowers to make an ounce," he notes. "How do I know this? I study and give my staff, waiters, and hostesses a quiz each week. We learn together about the ingredients and the process. I think it helps everyone and it's a challenge."

Fresh pasta, such as his favorite made with saffron, is one of Bomparola's specialties, but he insists that pasta is only part of his genuine Northern Italian cuisine. "Everyone thinks of Italian food as pasta, but in Italy, pasta is a side dish or an interlude between other courses," he points out. "The Italians eat several courses, but the plates are smaller. Here we eat huge bowls of a single pasta with some meat or chicken or fish added. That's not Italian."

Northern Italian features less reliance on sauces. Bomparola evokes his Milanese background with recipes for risotto, gnocchi, and polenta, and uses wood-fired rotisseries and grills to add flavor to seafood, beef, game, and poultry.

The atmosphere at Canaletto is relaxed, as befits the "outdoor" piazza in St. Mark's Square in the Grand Canal Shoppes at the Venetian. Close your eyes and you really are in Venice. Music floats in the air as entertainers sing and dance in the square. Gondolas slide through the canal, their guides crooning Italian love songs to hand-holding tourists. Inside, luxurious booths provide an intimate feeling under 16-foot ceilings.

"We do not rush diners," says Bomparola. "I enjoy seeing the smiles of satisfaction as customers enjoy the openness of the piazza and the relaxing comfort of the booths. It's all part of the worldly experience of eating at Canaletto. I want them to relish the taste in their mouths and the view from their seats."

Lobster and Dover Sole

Serves 4

Lobster and dover sole

4 4-oz.	fresh dover sole or halibut filets
4 large	individual lobster tails, raw
4 slices	Prosciutto di Parma
4 oz.	baby maché or lettuce leaf
1 cup	saffron rice
4 sprigs	thyme for garnish

Sauce

2 tbsp.	olive oil
8	baby artichokes, quartered
12	cherry tomatoes, quartered
8 small	white or yellow potatoes, boiled baby carrots
1/2 cup	white wine
1 large	lemon, squeezed
1 tbsp.	butter

For the lobster and dover sole:

• Cut the fish and wrap it around the lobster tail, with tail sticking up.
• Take the piece of prosciutto and wrap it horizontally around the fish leaving the top half of the fish exposed.
• Heat the olive oil in a sauce pan until hot.
• With tongs, place the fish in the pan and cook for 3 minutes on each side.
• Remove fish from sauce pan and place in a 350° oven for 4 minutes.
• Keep warm in a 200° oven while making the sauce.

For the sauce:

• Add 2 tablespoons of olive oil to sauté pan.
• Heat oil and sauté baby artichokes for 2 minutes.
• Add the cherry tomatoes to the sauté pan.
• Add potatoes and baby carrots.
• Continue to cook, stirring occasionally.
• Add the white wine and lemon juice. Reduce by one-third. Add the butter and whisk to thicken the sauce.

To complete:

• Place the cooked fish with the lobster tail up, in center of plate.
• Place the artichokes, potatoes, and carrots around the fish.
• Drizzle the sauce around the base of the fish and vegetables.
• Place the saffron rice beside the lobster tail, accenting with a sprig of thyme.
• Garnish the plate with the baby maché.

Wine pairing:

• King Estate Pinot Gris

Saffron Pasta and Seafood Luigi

Serves 2

Seafood

1/3 cup	olive oil
1 tsp.	garlic, crushed
8 large	shrimp, peeled, de-veined, size 16/20
6 medium	scallops on the shell
6 medium	scallops, size 20/30
6 large	Mediterranean black mussels
1/2 cup	white wine
1/3 cup	clam juice
1 pinch	salt
1 pinch	pepper
1 cup	leeks, fried
4	Roma tomatoes, sliced
1 lb.	fresh saffron pasta

For the seafood:
• In a hot sauté pan with the olive oil, add the garlic, shrimp, scallops, and mussels for 3 minutes.
• When the mussels open, add the wine and simmer for 30 seconds.
• Add the clam juice, salt and pepper.
• Remove from heat and reserve.

For the pasta:
• In a large pot, bring water to boil.
• Add the salt and fresh pasta and cook for 6-8 minutes, until tender.

To complete:
• Toss seafood with pasta and arrange in two dinner bowls.
• Garnish with the sliced tomatoes and fried leeks on top.

Wine pairing:
• Bourdeaux White 2002; Mission St. Vincent

Steve Blandino

2004 Award of Excellence, Wine Spectator

Just because the word "steak" appears in the name of the Charlie Palmer Steak restaurant at the award-winning Four Seasons Las Vegas doesn't mean that Executive Chef Steve Blandino doesn't have a few other tricks up his sleeve. Sure, his black Angus 21-day dry-aged beef is spectacular and has the critics salivating. The juicy cuts-like-butter wood-grilled filet mignon has been called the best steak in Las Vegas.

But Blandino is a chef, after all, and the cuisine he creates to surround those steaks is also spectacular. Take, for example, the crisp oysters with truffle-scented potato salad or the wild mushrooms with caramelized onions. This is a man who knows his way around the stove.

Introduced by a friend to Charlie Palmer, who has a reputation for enjoying mentoring young chefs, the handsome young Blandino worked for 18 months at Charlie Palmer's first Las Vegas restaurant, Aureole, before donning the toque at Charlie Palmer Steak in the Four Seasons. "The place was all set up; I have just worked into it and am putting my mark on it," says Blandino. "I credit Charlie Palmer with training us well and then having the confidence to give us the freedom to grow and go on to do what we do best."

Although Blandino says that if he hadn't become a chef he might have been a stockbroker, there probably wasn't ever much chance of that. He started cooking at age seven with his Italian grandmother in Brooklyn. "My mom worked and my grandmother was always in the kitchen," he recalls. "She would have me stirring or fetching or peeling, and that's where my love for the kitchen comes from. I love mixing things up."

After graduating from the Culinary Institute of America in New Hyde Park in upstate New York, Blandino worked in all types of restaurants and culinary environments, from a small French bistro on Long Island to a catering company, which, he says, "gave me a good introduction into volume and control with quality presentations." He notices that there's a difference between American-trained and European-trained chefs. "Chefs in the U.S. are more willing to take risks," he says. "In Europe they are more old-school."

Although he's constantly on the lookout for interesting recipes, his creative juices start to flow when he thinks about how he can change what he finds. "I read cookbooks and watch cooking shows, and then I ponder how I would do it differently," he confesses. "Sometimes I think about the dish and how it would be with a substitute product, such as lamb instead of pork or fish instead of chicken. Sometimes it's the seasoning to bring out a different flavor."

Tuna and different meats are some of his favorite ingredients. "I use very light spices to accent the natural flavor," Blandino explains. "I never want the diner to taste the food and think, 'Oh, rosemary,' instead of 'Ummmm, meat.'"

Blandino's goal as a chef is to "help train future chefs, exceed the expectations of our guests, and help our local farmers by using their products."

There's a clubby intimate atmosphere at Charlie Palmer Steak, whether you dine in the more formal main room with its warm ochre walls accented by dark mahogany or enjoy a light snack or after-dinner drink in the informal lounge, where overstuffed chairs and couches invite you to settle in to listen to live entertainment on Friday and Saturday evenings.

Carpaccio of Beef

with tiny salad, olive tapenade, and aged balsamic vinegar

Serves 4

Carpaccio of beef

4 4-oz.	dry-aged beef tenderloin
1 oz.	ground fennel seed
1 oz.	ground black pepper
1 oz.	ground coriander
1 oz.	nicoise olives
1 oz.	lucques olives
1 oz.	kalamata olives
2 oz.	parmesan reggiano
2 tbsp.	aged balsamic vinegar
1 bunch	frisee, or chickory, escarole, curly endive
1 cup	baby mixed greens
1 medium	french baguette, sliced thin and toasted
ground cayenne pepper to taste	

For the carpaccio:

- Dust the filet mignon with a blend of ground fennel seeds, coriander, black and cayenne peppers.
- Sear at very high heat on all sides as quickly as possible to ensure that it does not exceed a true "rare" temperature.
- Remove the beef and store it in the freezer long enough for it to set up and be sliced on the slicer to a paper-thin consistency.

For the olive tapenade:

- Use only the finest olives (nicoise, kalamata, and lucques) to make the olive tapenade.
- After pitting, blend the olives in a food processor with olive oil, chopped fresh garlic, salt and pepper, red wine vinegar, and a touch of hot chili pepper until it's easy to spread but not necessarily a purée.
- The tapenade is later spread on thin slices of toasted French baguette.

To complete:

- For the presentation of the dish, carefully layer the slices of beef on the plate so that they overlap slightly and complete a uniform full circle.
- The tiny salad consists of mixed baby greens and frisee, which is tossed with a simple red wine vinaigrette.
- Garnish the plate with the toast points, shaved parmesan reggiano, and aged balsamic vinegar.

Wine pairing:

- Fiano di Avellino, Feudi di San Gregorio, Friuli, Italy, 2001

Oven-Roasted Alaskan Halibut

with peas, seasonal mushrooms and pancetta sauce

Serves 4

Fish

4 6-oz.	Alaskan halibut filets
1 cup	fresh English peas, shelled
2 cups	pancetta lardons or high-quality bacon product
2 cups	golden chanterelles, Oregon morels, or other fresh seasonal mushrooms
1 sprig	fresh thyme
2-1/2 cups	chicken stock
3 cups	fresh spinach leaves
2 cups	leeks, sliced on diagonal
1/2 cup	micro greens
1 cup	butter, melted and browned

salt and pepper to taste

For the garnish:
• Place spinach, leeks, 1/2 cup of the chicken stock, and 1 tablespoon butter into a saucepan, and cook slowly until leeks are tender.
• Shell and blanch the peas until just tender. Sauté the mushrooms until lightly browned.

For the halibut:
• Season the fresh halibut with salt and pepper.
• Baste with brown butter, fresh thyme sprigs, and lemon juice.
• Cook in 350° oven for 3-5 minutes until done. Check tenderness with fork.

For the pancetta sauce:
• Cut the pancetta into small pieces and purée with 2 cups chicken stock, strain through a chinois, and place in a saucepan, cooking slowly until thickened.

To complete:
• Place the halibut atop a bed of sautéed baby spinach and leeks. Garnish the plate with the peas and mushrooms.
• Finish with micro greens to the side on the plate.

Wine pairing:
• Chassagne-Montrachet, Cru Maltroie, Colin Deleger, Burgundy, France, 2000

Helene An

Pass through the massive carved bronze doors of Crustacean in the Desert Passage Mall at the Aladdin and you enter the romantic sensuous world of French Colonial Vietnam. Draped banquettes and private dining rooms with balconies hint at private assignations. The burble of a Zen water garden invites Asian tranquility. Giant murals, original art, and a red lacquered dance floor recall the heydays of Le Metropole, the fashionable Hanoi supper club that drew diplomats, conspirators, and foreign correspondents, along with the grandparents of owner and Executive Chef Helene An.

"My daughter, Elizabeth, flung herself into designing this space," says An. "She wanted to recreate the feeling of legendary international nightspots where the famous and infamous dined in elegance and privacy." Dramatic lighting highlights dragon-patterned silk upholstery, carved wood, and the five antique opium beds imported from northern China that have been converted into dining spaces.

Helene An, who grew up in an aristocratic family in Hanoi, is the matriarch of a restaurant family that began with her mother, Diana, and extends to her five daughters, Hannah, Monique, Jacqueline, Catherine, and Elizabeth. When she came to the United States more than 30 years ago, she had little but a strong work ethic and family pride. "It took many many years to prove myself as a chef and a business woman," says An. "One has to love working with the food. You do not become a chef for the money. When the guests tell me how good they feel after eating one of our dishes, that compliment is the ultimate reward."

The food at Crustacean Las Vegas, the latest of the An family restaurants that include Crustacean Beverly Hills and Crustacean San Francisco, offers the same subtle blending of French and Vietnam flavors and textures.

The underlying philosophy, according to An, is the yin and yang of cooking—the balance of complex flavors with lightness and freshness. "I love fresh herbs and spices," she says. "Eating healthy is very important to me." For example, she uses shallots to increase circulation, chives to help respiration, dill to reduce high blood pressure, turmeric to cleanse, and other Vietnamese herbs such as Vietnamese basil, *tia-to,* and *rau ram* to increase digestion.

The use of those herbs and spices—think of lemongrass, mint, orange, soy, and ginger, for example—is what makes the food at Crustacean so special. In fact, the "Secret Kitchen," a sealed kitchen within the main kitchen which is accessible only to An family members, is the site of certain recipe preparations that An considers her family legacy.

But customers interested in recreating Crustacean's flavors will find Crustacean spices and sauces, along with frozen appetizers, at gourmet and specialty food markets. "You can take any of my sauces and mix them to create your own," says An. "Rub the combination into the bird, use it as a marinade for the meat, or add some to enhance a simple stock."

Although the An family has been delighting diners for 32 years, the dynasty shows no signs of dying out. Helene's daughters are daily involved in the business, and the grandchildren are being groomed. "My grandchildren want to cook with Grandma," says An. "I tell them to think about what foods they like, and how it tastes, and then we create their own dish. This is the next generation, learning as I did."

Steamed Flounder

with ginger, leek, and scallions

Serves 4

Fish

1/2 lbs.	fresh filet of fish (sea bass, flounder, etc.)
4	shiitake mushrooms, julienne
1/4	onions, julienne
1/2	leek, julienne
3-4	green onions (white only) julienne
3 bunch	dill (optional)
4 tsp.	soy sauce
4 tsp.	sesame oil
4 tsp.	olive oil
3 tsp.	salt
3 tsp.	pepper

For the flounder:

- Rinse the fish and pat dry.
- Marinate the fish with salt and pepper for 15 minutes.
- Place the fish in the center of a big piece of foil.
- Cover with mixture of onion, shiitake mushrooms, and ginger, soy sauce, sesame oil, and olive oil.
- Wrap the fish with foil and leave open a little bit.
- Put in a roasting pan with 1 cup of water and steam in a preheated 350° oven about 15 to 20 minutes.

To complete:

- Remove and put on serving plate.
- Sauté the leek and green onions very quickly and place on top of the fish and serve.

Wine pairing:

- The Brancott Reserve, Marlborough 2203—a Sauvignon Blanc from New Zealand

Roasted Poussin

with herbs and Granny Smith apple glaze

Serves 4

Poussin

4 1-1/2-lb.	poussins (small hens)
4 tbsp.	olive oil
4 tbsp.	parsley, chopped
4 tbsp.	basil, chopped
4 tbsp.	garlic, chopped
4 tbsp.	marjoram, chopped
4 tsp.	oregano
4 tsp.	ginger
4 tsp.	cilantro

Granny Smith apple glaze

4 cups	apple cider
8 tbsp.	honey
8 tbsp.	brown sugar
4 pieces	anise (optional)
2 tsp.	coriander (optional)
2 pieces	cinnamon
4 medium	Granny Smith apples, sliced
2 tsp.	salt
2 tsp.	cayenne

Preparing the poussins:
• Heat the olive oil in a sauté pan and cook the herbs about 2 minutes.
• Remove from heat and let cool.
• Rub over and under the skin of the poussins and inside the poussins.

Roasting the poussins:
• Preheat the oven for 15 minutes at 350°.
• Place the poussins on the roasting rack in a roasting pan. Add 1/2 cup of water to the roasting pan.
• Roast for 1/2 hour.

For finishing the Granny Smith apple glaze:
• Combine all ingredients in a saucepan and reduce.
• When it becomes syrupy, strain out solids and reserve.

To complete and serve the entrée:
• Remove the poussins from the oven and brush them with the glaze.
• Return them to the oven for 1 minute. Serve with your choice of vegetables such as mushrooms and sweet peas.

Wine pairing:
• ZD Pinot Noir 2001 from Carneros

Jean Joho

When you hear the words "child prodigy," you might think of Mozart or Mendelssohn or Paganini. But one day the list might include the name of French-born Jean Joho, who entered the kitchen at the tender age of six to peel veggies in his aunt's restaurant and found his life's work. Fast forward to a few years ago: Joho's Brassierre Jo restaurant was named James Beard Foundation's "1996 Best New Restaurant—Midwest" and Bon Appetit's "Best Chef of the Year."

But even prodigies have to put in their time rising to stardom. "When I was 13, I went to an auberge in Alsace to apprentice with Paul Haeberlin," says Joho. Stints in kitchens in Italy and Switzerland followed. "I studied for years," he says. "In Europe you cannot be a chef in 18 months. You have to travel and work with many great chefs for many many years to become great yourself."

At the ripe old age of 23, Joho had already become sous chef at a Michelin three-star restaurant, supervising a staff of 35. He further honed his skills at the Hotel Restaurant School in Strasbourg.

Today, Joho divides his time between the various restaurants he has opened: Everest in Chicago atop the Chicago Stock Exchange, Brasserie Jo in Chicago and Boston, and Eiffel Tower at Paris Las Vegas. "Each restaurant has its own personality—the neighborhood, the people, the fresh products available in the area," says Joho, sounding like a proud papa. "I love blending the combinations of food with the restaurant's personality. I like visiting my 'children' around the country."

He calls his award-winning food "updated classical French." By that he means he starts with the basics of French cooking and adds his own touches—a talent for juxtaposing unexpected flavors to create a highly personalized cuisine. For example, imagine caviar paired with cauliflower. The combination wowed *Wine Spectator*, which referred to its "dazzling flavors." Or conjure up a pot-au-feu of rutabaga, sauerkraut, and brussel sprouts with tenderloin filets.

Asked what his favorite dish is, the elegant silvery-haired gentleman looks horrified. "I have no favorite dishes!" he exclaims. "How can you have a favorite 'child'? I love all my dishes. I don't serve anything I don't like."

Joho's imagination is stimulated by the ingredients and products themselves. He also reads cookbooks. "Sometimes I find a new idea in an old book," he says. "I read cookbooks in many different languages, and that is inspiring."

Joho has a passion and reverence for the culinary masters who have come before him and the history he hopes to make in his own way. "I enjoy watching my young cooks grow and learn and become successful," he says, "whether they open their own pizza shop or bistro or become an executive chef somewhere."

And he has a passion for his guests. "I want to give them the best experience," he says. "They are putting great trust in me when they choose my restaurant. My food is about enjoying the moment of dining—the togetherness and convivial nature of fine food and great company. Life without food is boring."

Dining at Eiffel Tower is anything but boring. Start with the 340-foot-per-minute ride up the center of the tower in a wedge-shaped glass elevator. Then enjoy the view of Bellagio's dancing fountains or the distant mountains beyond the neon Strip. It may not be Paris, France, but it comes pretty close.

Eiffel Tower Lobster Thermidor

Serves 4

4 1-1/2-lb.	live lobsters
6 oz.	spinach
2 tbsp.	olive oil
1 clove	garlic, chopped
6 oz.	wild mushrooms
2 small	shallots, finely chopped
1/2 cup	lobster sauce
1	egg yolk
1/2 cup	whipped cream
1/4 cup	grated parmesan cheese
2 tbsp.	bread crumbs
1 bunch	baby watercress
1 pinch	paprika

For preparing the lobsters:

- Place lobsters in a large stock pot of salted water.
- Cook for approximately 4-5 minutes. Remove from pot with tongs and place in ice water to stop the cooking process.
- Cut lobsters in half lengthwise and remove lobster meat from claw and tails, reserving shells.
- Quickly sauté spinach with the olive oil and garlic. Season with salt and pepper, then set aside.
- Clean and dice mushrooms, sauté with shallots, season with salt and pepper, then set aside. Fill the lobster bodies with spinach and mushrooms, top with the lobster meat, and heat an oven at 375° for approximately 3 minutes.
- Mix lobster sauce with egg yolk and whipped cream. Season to taste. Remove the lobsters from the oven.
- Ladle sauce on top of the lobster meat. Sprinkle paprika and bread crumbs and place under the broiler until golden brown.
- Transfer onto plates, then garnish with paprika and watercress.

Wine pairing:

- Josmeyer Tokay Pinot Gris Brand, 2001

Eiffel Tower Chocolate Soufflé

Serves 4

6 oz.   dark sweet chocolate, melted
1/2 cup   granulated sugar
1/4 cup   flour
1 cup   milk
1 tbsp.   butter
4 large   egg yolks
1 tbsp.   vanilla
1 tbsp.   espresso, room temperature
6   egg whites
confectioners sugar for the top

To complete the chocolate soufflé:
- Preheat the oven to 400°.
- Butter four 4-oz. soufflé dishes.
- Sprinkle each soufflé dish with granulated sugar, shaking out the excess.
- In a bowl, whisk together 1/4 cup of the granulated sugar, the flour, and 1/3 cup of the milk.
- Scald the remaining milk in a saucepan and add it to the bowl in a stream, whisking, until the mixture is smooth.
- Transfer the mixture to a saucepan; whisking continuously, bring to a simmer. Cook, continuing to whisk for 3 minutes or until thick. Remove the pan from the heat and beat in the butter.
- Beat in the egg yolks, one yolk at a time, then the vanilla, melted chocolate, and espresso. In a separate bowl with an electric mixer, beat the egg whites until they hold stiff peaks.
- Add the remaining granulated sugar, a little at a time to the egg whites, and beat until the whites hold stiff peaks.
- Stir 1/4 of the whites into the chocolate mixture, then fold in the remaining whites gently but thoroughly.
- Spoon the mixture into the prepared soufflé dish.
- Place the soufflé in the oven and immediately reduce the oven temperature to 375°.
- Bake the soufflé for 35 to 40 minutes, or until puffed.
- Sift the confectioner's sugar over the top and serve the soufflé at once.

Serve with vanilla sauce

DIFFICULTY LEVEL: 3

Anthony Amoroso

New York City born-and-bred Anthony Amoroso was chugging along as a freshman in college, thinking about science, and wondering if his future included marine biology. But his mother knew him better and suggested cooking school.

"I didn't even know about cooking schools at that point in my life," says Amoroso. But since he'd always loved cooking for his family, he enrolled. "The first day they gave me chef whites and told us what type of shoes to buy," he adds. "They said that the next day we would get knives. At that moment, I was totally sucked in. The magic struck and I've never looked back."

The magic also strikes those who eat his sophisticated interpretations of simple Italian food at this sister restaurant to the Soho, New York, original. "The idea is to introduce new foods in a way that's fun and doesn't offend anyone," he says. "I had a gentleman from the Midwest tell me this was the first time he had ever eaten octopus and he loved it."

Amoroso, who began his career at New York's Oceana and R. M., both three-star restaurants, comes at food with a scientist's mind. "When I was starting out, I used to get upset when clients didn't understand what I was trying to do with textures and aromas," he explains. "Now I understand that not everyone cares about the science as I do. They're just happy to have a pleasing food experience."

To deliver that experience, Amoroso has definite standards. Temperature, for example, is important to him. "Food is best served at a little above room temperature, because it allows the flavors to develop in your mouth," he explains. He also thinks about taste as a series of layers. "It's the acidity that makes the food taste great," he adds. "Spice generates the heat making the food feel alive in our mouths. It's also important to have underlying notes that are nutty to bring a finish to the bite. Aroma is often the background note, and that's added to by the wine."

Seasonings play an important role in every dish he creates and he's very particular about what he uses. "As a cook you should understand what you're trying to accomplish, how you're going to get there, and what the experience should be to the diner," he notes. "I like fennel seed and pepperoncino (red chili flakes). I use kosher salt, fine sea salt, and gray salt. I don't use a lot of garlic because garlic is used with tomato-based Southern Italian cooking to attract the sweet tastiness of the tomato. I like to balance that sweet and sour by using different vinegars and sugar."

Amoroso enjoys training his staff in his principles and techniques. "I'm very close in age, at thirty, to my staff, so there's a common thread in our thinking," he says. "I like exposing everyone in the kitchen to new techniques and experiences. My great grandmother always says, 'The talent is in your hands.'

Fiamma means "flame" in Italian; at MGM Grand in Las Vegas it burns with cool chic. A four-sided glass fireplace blazes with a blue and gold gas-light flame. A mixture of new age, jazz, and instrumental music fills the air. Woven gunmetal gray columns set off sienna walls and copper porcupines cast muted light around the room. A combination of teak, marble, and leather creates a cozy den-like feel. It's the perfect setting to mellow out with great Italian food.

Grilled Branzino

(Mediterranean sea bass)
with braised artichokes and lemon

Serves 4

Sea bass

4 8-oz.	sea bass filets (black sea bass or striped bass can be used, as well as any lean white fish, i.e. snapper or grouper)
2 cups	leaf spinach or arugula, loosely packed, washed, dried
1/4 cup	extra virgin olive oil
1 large	lemon cut in quarters, seeds removed
1 bunch	flat-leaf parsley leaves, picked and chopped
4 parts	braised artichokes (recipe follows)
4 parts	artichoke purée (recipe follows)

kosher salt or fine sea salt to taste
fresh ground pepper to taste

Braised artichokes

4 large	artichokes (leaves peeled and choke removed; store in 2 quarts water with the juice of 2 lemons added to prevent browning)
1 large	white onion, peeled, halved, and sliced thin
1 large	carrot, peeled, split lengthwise, and sliced across thin
1 stalk	celery, split lengthwise and sliced thin on a bias
1 bulb	fennel, halved and sliced thin
1 cup	dry white wine
5 sprigs	thyme
2 leaves	fresh bay leaf or 1 dry
1 pinch	red chili flakes
1 cup	extra virgin olive oil

Artichoke purée

1 pint	artichoke stems, removed from the braised artichokes
1/4 cup	lemon juice
1/4 cup	artichoke cooking liquid

salt and pepper to taste
Add all ingredients to a blender, purée until smooth, and reserve.

For the artichokes:

• Preheat a 4- to 6-quart pot over medium low heat and add olive oil.
• Add onion, celery, fennel, carrot, and sweat until vegetables begin to soften.
• Strain artichokes, reserving the liquid, and add the artichokes to the pot.
• Sauté lightly, stirring frequently until onions are translucent, then add the herbs and spices and season with salt to taste.
• Add white wine and bring to a simmer, then add just enough of the reserved lemon water to cover the artichokes and bring to a slow simmer.
• Simmer until the artichokes are fork tender, about 30 to 45 minutes.
• Transfer the contents of the pot to a large mixing bowl and refrigerate until cool.
• Once cool, cut away the stems and reserve for purée and cut the artichoke hearts into quarters and return to the vegetables and liquid for storage.

Note: The artichokes, once cool, can be packed with their liquid and vegetables in an airtight container and stored for up to 1 week in the refrigerator.

To complete the entrée:

• Pre-heat a grill to medium heat and brush the sea bass filets with olive oil and season with salt.
• Proceed to grill the filets on the skin side only until just cooked through, about 4 to 5 minutes per 1/2 inch of fish. If you do not have access to a grill, the filets can be sautéed.
• Remove from the grill onto a plate and squeeze the lemon quarters over the fish. Drizzle with a little fresh olive oil and sprinkle with the chopped parsley. Hold warm for plating.
• Reheat the artichoke hearts with their liquid and braising vegetables.
• On 4 warm dinner plates, divide the artichoke purée equally, top the purée with the warmed braised artichokes, sprinkle the plates with the arugula leaves, and top with the fish filets.
• Finish with a drizzle of lemon and olive oil.

Wine pairing:
• Gavi di Gavi
• Piedmonte 2002 La Scolca Black Label

DIFFICULTY LEVEL: 4   Chef Anthony Amoroso © 2005 Fiamma Trattoria

Charred Octopus Salad

Serves 2

Octopus

2 lbs.	small octopus
2 large	Idaho potatoes peeled, diced small, blanched until tender, and reserved
1 large	red bell pepper, roasted, peeled, seeded, and sliced
1 head	frisee lettuce, cleaned, and snipped into pieces
1/2 bunch	mint leaves

Octopus poaching liquid

2 quarts	water
1/2 cup	red-wine vinegar
10 pcs.	black peppercorn
1 tbsp.	kosher salt
2 ea.	fresh bay leaf
1 pinch	chili flake

Octopus marinade

1 cup	extra virgin olive oil
1 each	lemon, sliced
1 each	orange, sliced
2 cloves	garlic, split in half
2 sprigs	rosemary
2 sprigs	thyme
1 pinch	chili flakes
1 pinch	kosher salt (Diamond Crystal)

Lemon mint vinaigrette

1 oz.	lemon juice
2 oz.	red-wine vinegar
1 each	shallot, diced fine
1 tsp.	Dijon mustard
1 cup	extra virgin olive oil
1/2 bunch	mint leaves, picked
1 pinch	chili flakes
fine sea salt to taste	

Olive pesto (optional)

1/2 pint	pitted green olives
1 tbsp.	pine nuts
1/4 cup	extra virgin olive oil
1/4 cup	flat-leaf parsley, leaves picked
1/4 cup	mint leaves, picked
1/4 cup	basil leaves, picked
1 tsp.	capers, rinsed
1 clove	garlic, roasted
zest and juice of 1 lemon	
salt and fresh ground black pepper to taste	

For the poaching liquid:

• Combine all poaching liquid ingredients in a large pot and bring to a simmer. Add the octopus, gently simmer for 1-1/2 hours, and remove the octopus to a large mixing bowl.

For the marinade:

• Combine all the marinade ingredients in a large bowl, pour over the warm poached octopus, and place in the refrigerator to cool.

For the vinaigrette:

• Place all the ingredients in a blender and purée until incorporated.

For the olive pesto:

• Combine all the ingredients in a food processor, except the olive oil, and purée until smooth. Scrape down the sides of the bowl and continue to purée with machine running slow.
• Add olive oil until incorporated, season to taste, and refrigerate for up to 1 week.

Finish the entrée:

• Preheat a grill or large skillet on high heat.
• Remove the octopus from the marinade and split in half lengthwise to remove the beak. Cut the octopus again into quarters and char on all sides over the grill or in the skillet.
• Once charred, remove to a large mixing bowl and add the peppers, mint leaves, and frisee, drizzle with the lemon mint vinaigrette, and toss well.
• Then, in another bowl, combine the cooked potatoes and 2 tablespoons of the pesto, if using; otherwise add the potatoes to the bowl containing the octopus salad.
• If using the pesto potatoes, divide the potatoes amongst 4 plates and top with the octopus salad. Otherwise, divide the salad with the plain potatoes amongst the plates and serve immediately.
• To garnish, drizzle with a little fresh olive oil and more mint leaves.

Wine pairing:

• Piedmonte 2002 La Scolca Black Label

Marc Poidevin

Marc Poidevin was born in Montauban in southwest France, where his parents owned a catering business. Rabbit, duck, and foie gras were an integral part of his life. "I learned how to butcher, clean fish, and cook from a very young age," he says. "The artistic and creative side of me came out in the kitchen."

Thus, it was no surprise when, at 15, he went off to cooking school in Paris. "The school was very very hard," he remembers. "The masters demanded that you be precise, quick, and accurate. I memorized the recipes and had to execute them on demand. But every student came away bulletproof." He received a double degree, one in classic French cuisine, the other in restaurant management.

After graduation, he refined his French cooking skills in the kitchen of the famous chef Roger Verge at the Moulin de Mougin on the French Riviera. It didn't take him long to be promoted to sous chef.

So it's no wonder that when this energetic Frenchman came to America, he brought *haute cuisine francaise* with him. It's not only in his blood, he's also a master at it.

"Actually, when I was young I wanted to be a veterinarian," he confesses. "But my grades were not so good." The world of foodies can be thankful for that. Poidevin has been collecting critical acclaim and awards for French food during his restaurant journey in the United States, which includes top restaurants in New York City and Florida. "Every chef I have ever worked with has influenced me," he says. And he's worked with some of the best. When he joined Sotha Khunn at the original Le Cirque in New York, the restaurant soared to national prominence.

Fame has followed him to Bellagio in Las Vegas, where his Le Cirque kitchen has been praised for a new standard of excellence. His philosophy of food is straightforward: "Keep it simple. Let the food come out." One of his favorite ingredients is truffles—black or white. "This year I went to hunt the black truffle. It was fantastic," he says. "I hope to go again when the white truffle is in season." Truffles adorn such dishes as truffle-roasted salmon, white-truffle risotto, and sea scallops with black truffle and spinach in puff pastry.

Poidevin finds inspiration from books. "I love to collect very old cookbooks from all over the world," he says. "I watch the combinations of ingredients. Sometimes what is old becomes new again." And new, within the French classic tradition, is what he is constantly seeking: "I am intense and always excited by discovering new things," he says. "There are no limits to the creative ability to do this job I love."

If he could go back in time, Poidevin says he'd love to talk to Georges-Auguste Escoffier, the French chef from the London Savoy Hotel at the turn of the 19th century. "He wrote the book, literally the *Dictionary of Food*," says Poidevin. "It holds all the secrets, the definitions and descriptions for every type of food, recipe, and technique. I would like to ask Escoffier what has changed. Is it time to be rewritten? Maybe that will be my next career challenge."

Dining beside Bellagio's dancing waters under the whimsical striped-silk circus-tent ceiling in Le Cirque is festive. But although the décor creates a sense of excitement, the classic French food of Marc Poidevin is always in the center ring.

Black Truffle Chicken

Serves 2

Chicken

1 2-lb.	whole chicken
1 head	garlic
8 sprigs	thyme
1 tsp.	truffle oil
12 slices	black truffle
2 tbsp.	olive oil
salt and pepper	

Chicken sauce

1 lb.	chicken bones
1 head	garlic
1 cup	white wine
4 small	shallots, sliced
1 quart	chicken stock
1 tsp.	truffle oil
1/2 cup	truffle juice
2 tbsp.	whole butter
salt and pepper	

Garnish

1 cup	fresh peas
1 oz.	fresh foie gras
8 pc.	lardon or diced bacon
1	black truffle, sliced thin
8 pc.	porcini, sliced
10 pc.	Yukon Gold potatoes, tourné
4 sprigs	fresh parsley
1 pinch	rock salt

For the chicken sauce:
- Roast the chicken bones for 30 minutes at 375° or until brown.
- Add garlic and shallots. Then deglaze with the white wine.
- Add chicken stock and simmer for one hour.
- Pass through a chinoise, then discard the solids.
- Finish with the truffle oil, truffle peelings, and truffle juice.
- Add butter away from the heat and whisk until slightly thickened.

For the black truffle chicken:
- Season inside of the chicken with salt, pepper, crushed garlic cloves, and thyme sprigs.
- Lift skin of the chicken and arrange a layer of truffles under the skin. Rub the skin with black-truffle oil and season.
- Roast in a 350° oven for 25 minutes until golden brown and juices are clear.
- De-bone the chicken and slice the meat.

To complete:
- Roast the porcini mushrooms with chicken livers and lardon.
- Blanche the peas, and add to the mushroom mixture.
- Add the chicken sauce, chopped truffles, and simmer.
- Roast the Yukon Gold tourné potatoes until golden brown.
- Add roast potatoes to the sauce, then portion onto 4 warm plates.
- Arrange the sliced chicken on top of the truffle sauce and serve.

Wine pairing:
- Burgundy or Côte du R

Grilled John Dory Filet

with braised Napa cabbage and chorizo

Serves 2

Sauce

Bones of 1 John Dory, reserve the filets
2   shallots, sliced
1 sprig   fresh thyme
2 cups   red wine
1 cup   port wine
1 tbsp.   heavy cream
4 oz.   unsalted butter, softened
salt and freshly ground pepper

Garnish

2 tbsp.   unsalted butter
1 tbsp.   celery root, peeled, brunoise
1 tbsp.   carrot, peeled, brunoise
1 tbsp.   red onion, brunoise
1 tbsp.   chorizo sausage, brunoise
1 head   Napa cabbage,
            sliced 1/4" thick
1 tbsp.   yellow celery leaves, chopped
1 tbsp.   chives, chopped
1 medium   green apple, peeled
1 tbsp.   cider vinegar

John Dory

2 6-oz.   John Dory filets
sea salt and freshly ground pepper
1 tbsp.   extra virgin olive oil

For the sauce:

• Roast the John Dory bones in 375° oven until browned.
• Add shallots and thyme.
• Deglaze with red wine and port. Simmer until reduced to a syrup-like consistency. Strain through a fine chinoise and discard bones.
• Add the heavy cream and whisk in the butter.
• Season with salt and pepper to taste. Place in a warm location until you're ready to finish the entrée.

For the garnish:

• In a large pot over medium heat, cook the celery, carrot, onion, and chorizo in the butter, until tender, but not browned.
• Increase heat from medium to high and add the Napa cabbage. Cook until just wilted.
• Deglaze with the cider vinegar and cook until dry.
• Season to taste and keep warm.
• Using a small melon baller, make 20 tiny balls from the green apple.

For the John Dory:

• Season the fish filets lightly on both sides and rub with olive oil.
• Cook over a hot grill until the fish filets have just turned opaque in the center.

To complete the entrée:

• Divide the garnish onto two warm plates. Place the fish on top of the cabbage and drizzle the sauce around the fish.
• Top the fish with the green apple balls and the yellow celery leaves and serve.

Wine pairing:

• King Estate Pinot Noir from Oregon

Chef Marc Poidevin © 2005 Le Cirque Las Vegas

Marcus Ritz

Marc Ritz is one of those chefs who likes to come to the table and talk to his guests. "What do you feel like eating tonight?" he'll say. "I just got this new prosciutto in today from the Parma region in northern Italy. The pigs there are fed organic meals. And I have a 2000 parmesan cheese that's so dry it melts in your mouth. Or I have a soft provolone with truffle bits."

Well removed from the Vegas Strip, Marc's is an intimate warm place with innovative combinations of foods that caters to the local trade. "This is truly a neighborhood place where locals can feel comfortable," he says. You'll get a little touch of Thai, some Japanese, and a little French. And, of course, Italian. But after all, Ritz does call his food "world cuisine."

Hands-on experience rather than formal culinary school is how Ritz got his training. His first kitchen duty was rolling dough in his dad's pizzeria in upstate New York. "He taught me the technique and the flavors of my Italian heritage," he says. "My grandmother taught me, too."

But perhaps it's that very lack of rigid culinary education that makes him feel so free to experiment. "I try to create good food that has a unique twist," he explains. "Many times I'm unorthodox in my cooking principles. Adding cheese and capers to a marinara sauce is not considered authentic. But it works for everyone who has tasted it. I like my guests to be willing to let go of their regular favorites and try new things. That's the creativity I love."

He gets his ideas by watching the Travel Channel and going to the local market. In order to further his skills he did a stint in a Tuscan kitchen in Italy at one point and brought back an armload of new recipes. Other recipes have come from his travels to Thailand and various places around the globe. Wherever he goes, he learns about the food.

Seasonal products figure prominently in his dishes. "I want to know what place the food actually came from, how long ago, and how soon it will be here," he says. "Sometimes a guest will describe something and I get interested in trying to recreate it." He loves pasta and using fresh produce, a little basil, and extra virgin olive oil.

Ritz confesses that it was a craving for attention that made him become a chef. "I was a Golden Gloves fighter in my younger years," he boasts. "Now I spar three to four days a week, just to keep up my stamina. I love the gym almost as much as the kitchen."

But it was cooking that won his heart. "Cooking gave me the opportunity to put on a show and delight my friends and family," he says. "I love talking to the diners and sharing my knowledge. People like to know about the food, where it came from, how it's prepared—it improves their entire experience. The care and love that go into each dish make the guest feel involved and raise the expectation level. The attention the diner gets here is like no other place I know."

Ritz dreams of opening a true Italian market/deli. "It will be a place where you can buy the real deal," he says. "Then you can sit outside, sip a cappuccino, and eat a fresh-baked dessert."

Osso Buco

Serves 8

8 4-in.	veal shanks (with center bone)
1 cup	all-purpose flour
1 large	red onion
1 clove	garlic
1 bottle	white wine-24 oz. Chablis
4 tbsp.	tomato paste
2 tbsp.	Worcestershire
1-1/2 tsp.	Tabasco
1 tsp.	kosher salt
1-5	black peppercorns (medium grind)
1/2 tsp.	oregano
1 stem	thyme
1 stem	rosemary
1 cup	Romano cheese
1/2 lb.	roux
3 large	carrots, quartered
3 whole	celery sticks

For the osso buco:
- Flour the shanks and sear on both sides.
- Place in a deep roasting pan or oven-safe skillet.
- In same pan where shanks were seared, add onions and sweat them. Add garlic and white wine to deglaze.
- Add tomato paste, Worcestershire, Tabasco, salt, pepper, oregano, thyme, and rosemary.
- Stir constantly. Bring to a boil and add the cheese.
- Incorporate the roux and stir until smooth.
- Pour sauce over shanks, completely covering. Top with the carrots and celery sticks.
- Seal with aluminum foil.
- Bake at 225° for 6 hours or until tender (falling off the bone).

To complete:
- Arrange the veal shanks in a wide bowl with some of the sauce.

Wine pairing:
- Piemonte Nabbiolo Barolo

John Dory Piccata

Serves 4

John Dory

1 1/2 lb.	John Dory, skin on
1/2 cup	all-purpose flour
1 pinch	sea salt
1 pinch	black pepper
1/4 cup	olive oil
1 tsp.	unsalted butter
1 medium	lemon, sliced
1 dozen	capers

Sauce

1/2 cup	sherry, dry wine
1/2 cup	Chablis, white wine
4 oz.	unsalted butter
1 medium	lemon, halved
2 tbsp.	parsley, chopped

For the fish:

- Spread flour over work surface and season flour with salt and pepper.
- Cut the fish into 8 pieces, scoring the skin with a sharp knife. Coat the fish with flour and shake off excess.
- In a large sauté pan, heat the olive oil. Place fish into pan and brown.
- Add 1 tsp. unsalted butter to pan for better brown.
- Add 1 slice of lemon for each piece of fish and add the caper berries.
- Turn fish after 4 minutes of cooking and cook on the other side for another 4 minutes.
- Remove the fish from the pan and discard the oil.
- Place on a plate lined with paper towels to drain any excess oil.

For the sauce:

- Add both wines to the pan used to brown the fish.
- Add the remaining butter and squeeze half of remaining lemon into pan.
- Cook until butter is melted by swirling the pan for one minute.

To serve:

- Warm the plates.
- Ladle sauce onto each plate and carefully place fish into the sauce.
- Top with fresh chopped parsley.
- Place lemon section on side of plate and serve.

Wine pairing:

- Fiano di Avellino

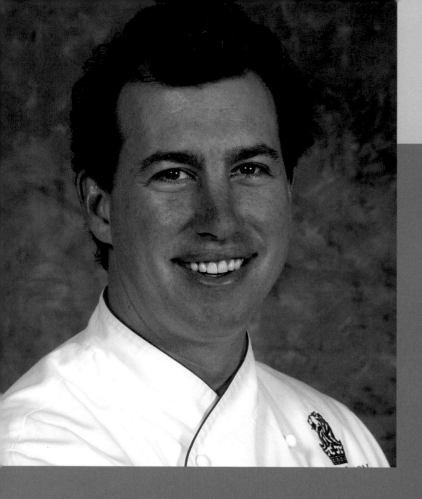

Stephen Marshall

He was young and he was one of two Americans on a Royal Viking Cruise slated to make port in 24 countries around the world. Stephen (pronounced Stehfan) Marshall recounts the glamour of it all: "I was the guy cleaning twenty cases of spinach every day in the kitchen." But he learned about different styles of food and he was exposed to more than 30 different cooks. "What I learned," he says, "is that as a chef, you never stop learning."

Not that Marshall was a stranger to the kitchen before voyaging around the world. "My father is a great gourmet, and he and I would cook dinner together at home," he says. His father encouraged him to get a job in a restaurant kitchen. One day, Chef Roberto Gerometta made a meal for the new worker in his kitchen.

"I saw how it was so artistically done," recalls Marshall. "That was the beginning for me. At that moment, I said to myself, 'I can do this!' I knew I wanted to do something exciting and creative. I immediately set my sights on converting my energy into becoming a chef."

Marshall likens being a chef to being a craftsman. "You have to spend a lot of time cooking and thinking about food," he says. "It's a passion that occupies twelve to fourteen hours of the day. You cannot become a chef by reading a book. You have to live it, feel it, breathe it." In the 20 years of his working life, Marshall has had only one Christmas off. "That was when I came here and the hotel was not open yet," he notes. "I love what I do, so the time flies."

For more than 13 years, Marshall has worked in Ritz-Carlton kitchens around the world. Teaching his cooks what he knows is a responsibility he takes seriously. "I'm their information center," he states. "I am cultivating the chefs." He loves the ambience of the kitchen. "Being in the kitchen is like performing an extraordinary dance. In the heat of the action, people are moving around you, behind you, on top; you have a rhythm," he says. "When we all understand our roles and feel the momentum, the pace is exhilarating, because the timing is precise and it all flows."

Marshall began cooking Italian food, which he calls perfect, simple, yet flavorful. "I love tomatoes, and fruits and vegetables that are live with color, taste, and texture," he says. "Fish is alive. I like the balance of sweetness and acidity when you mix different products in the freshness of that season."

For home cooks, Marshall shares this advice: "To cook a dish properly, you need the best ingredients—the freshest fish and the right spices. Concentrate on what you are doing. Put a lot of passion into it and enjoy the process. Don't cook if you don't feel like it—it takes the fun out of it and more than likely you won't get a good product. Go out of the box. Look for the easy things to do, because too many instructions won't be fun and you'll be too tired to enjoy. Go for the simple pleasures."

The Medici Café is a perfect partner for Marshall's food—both are elegant, yet relaxed. Fresh flowers and Renaissance art add romance indoors, or diners may choose to sit and view the Florentine gardens outside the Las Vegas Ritz.

Veal and Ahi Tuna Spirals

with leek polenta tart, lemon-caper-butter sauce

Serves 6

Veal and ahi tuna spirals

6 3-oz.	blocks of ahi tuna
6 2-oz.	pieces of veal scallopine
olive oil	

Leek polenta tart

1 cup	leeks (white part only)
1 cup	polenta
3 cups	water
1 oz.	butter
3 oz.	mascarpone cheese

Caper lemon butter sauce

8 oz.	butter
1/2 cup	white wine
1 large	lemon, juiced
1 large	shallot, finely chopped
2 oz.	capers
1/4 cup	parsley, finely chopped
1 cup	veal stock

Garnish

1 box	fine watercress
1 cup	fava beans, cooked and cleaned

For the tart:

- In a large saucepan, add the leeks and butter, then cook for 10 minutes on low heat until the leeks are very soft.
- Add the polenta, olive oil, and water to the leeks and cook for 15-20 minutes on low flame until the grains are soft.
- Remove from heat and pour into a shallow pan. Let the polenta cool and cut into half moons.
- Sear the polenta and reserve until ready to serve.

For the veal and tuna spirals:

- Lay the veal scallopine down on a cutting board and place the cylinder of ahi on top, then roll and seal with a toothpick.
- Cook in olive oil and butter on medium heat until the tuna is medium rare, then remove from the pan.

For the sauce:

- While the pan is still hot, add the shallots and 1 tbsp. of the butter. Cook for 45 seconds and deglaze with the white wine. Reduce by half and add the veal stock and lemon juice.
- Cook until reduced by half. Finish the sauce with parsley and butter. Arrange the polenta and the veal and tuna spirals on the plate.
- Sprinkle fava beans around edge of plate. Garnish center with watercress, season, and serve.

Wine pairing:

- Robert Sinskey Pinot Noir 2001

Caramelized Onion and Artichoke Tart

with goat cheese and oven-dried tomatoes

Serves 6

Caramelized onions

2 large	onions, sliced fine
2 pieces	garlic, chopped fine
1/4 bunch	thyme
3 tbsp.	butter
1 tsp.	olive oil
3-4	green or black olives, for garnish

Tart

1/4 lb.	parmesan cheese, shaved thin
1/4 lb.	arugula, for garnish
2 whole	tomatoes, cut into petals and dried in the oven
2 sheets	puff pastry, cut into diamonds and baked (be sure to cut a 1/4-inch slit in pastry before cooking)
3 large	artichoke hearts with stems attached, cooked

Goat cheese

1 cup	goat cheese
3 tbsp.	cream
1/4 cup	finely grated parmesan cheese

For the goat cheese:
- Mix the ingredients together until smooth.

For the caramelized onions:
- In a large sauté pan sweat the onions with the garlic and thyme in the olive oil and butter over a low flame, stirring every 1-2 minutes. This process will take about 30 minutes and you should have well caramelized sweet onions. Remove and cool.

To complete:
- Remove the top of the puff pastry diamonds and fill with the caramelized onions, then top with the artichokes.
- Place in the oven for 2-3 minutes or until tart is hot.
- Place in the center of the plate and drizzle with olive oil.
- Top with shaved parmesan cheese and surround the dish with the goat cheese. Garnish with the olives and baby tomatoes.

Wine pairing:
- Cakebread Cellars Chardonnay 2002

Mimmo Ferraro

Mimmo Ferraro has inherited his father's good looks, but that's only one of the reasons locals, tourists, and celebrities flock to his restaurant. Visiting Mimmo Ferraro's, located on West Flamingo off the razzle-dazzle of the Vegas Strip, is like stopping at the home of an old family friend. The waiters make you feel as if you've been coming there for years. A band plays Frank Sinatra hits, setting the perfect mood for dancing in the intimate lounge. Dim lighting adds a touch of romance. "We do not rush our guest from the table," says Mimmo. "Many folks come to enjoy their evening with the music and the relaxing atmosphere."

But it's safe to say that while all the above make the restaurant a pleasant place to be, it's the food that really draws the customers and impresses the critics. Mimmo credits his grandmother, Teresa. "She gave my whole family the core values that include hard work, using only the best ingredients, and keeping the presentation simple. She has a family vault of recipes from Italy," he says.

Mimmo is the third generation of cooks in the Ferraro line. "Growing up, I loved the family meals we enjoyed together," he says. "I learned by watching my grandmother and my mother in the kitchen, then watching my dad."

His dad is Gino Ferraro, founder of the restaurant. Although Gino's early ambition was to open a chain of coffee cafes à la Starbucks, his first restaurant in Las Vegas was a pizzeria and deli. A course of study at the Italian Culinary

School in Soverato, Italy, under master chef Giovanni Gattis helped him to expand his dreams to fine Italian dining. In 1985 he began serving the family-heritage recipes to Las Vegas. The critics raved and the legend was launched.

The toque has now passed from father to son. Mimmo is up to the task. "I love the action and excitement of a busy night," he says. "I'm always ready to jump into the line and help prepare every dish before it's presented to the guest."

It's been reported that Julia Roberts leads a crowd of people who believe the gnocchi—light potato dumplings caressed with gorgonzola or Bolognese sauce—are the best to be had. Then there's the osso buco, veal shank in burgundy sauce, that has become the signature dish and boasts a Five Star Diamond Award.

Mimmo loves to try new twists on the traditional Italian dishes he's known all his life, and he enjoys it when a guest says, "Do something special." But it's hard to top the regular menu of homemade breads, pastas, seafood, and veal. Mimmo follows the family tradition of using only the freshest ingredients. His favorite dish is a bowl of fresh pasta dressed in Italian olive oil.

When not firing up the stove, Mimmo gets his adrenaline going with a workout at the gym. It keeps him at the top of his form. And after all, as a third-generation restaurateur with a kitchen full of family recipes, he has a lot to live up to. So far, he's doing just fine.

Veal Piemontese

Serves 2

Veal

4 1/4-in.	veal medallions
2 tbsp.	extra virgin olive oil
2 tsp.	butter
2 tsp.	gorgonzola cheese
2 tsp.	minced shallots
2 tsp.	sliced black truffles
1/2 cup	veal stock
salt and pepper	

For the veal:
- Pound the veal medallions to 1/4" thickness.
- In a sauté pan, heat olive oil over a high flame.
- Sauté veal medallions approximately 30 seconds per side. Discard the oil.
- Add butter, shallots, and cheese to pan and sauté for 30 seconds.
- Add brandy, truffles, and veal stock, then reduce by half, approximately 1-2 minutes.
- Season with salt and pepper.

To complete:
- Arrange the veal medallions on a plate and serve with your favorite vegetable.

Wine pairing:
- Brunello Dimonte, Montalgino, Super Tuscany

DIFFICULTY LEVEL: 2   Chef Mimmo Ferraro © 2005 Mimmo Ferraro's

Fusilli Aragosta

Serves 4

Lobster

2 tbsp.	extra virgin olive oil
4 4-oz.	lobster tails, shelled
1/4 cup	shallots, minced
1 cup	green peas
1 cup	lobster meat
1 cup	sun-dried tomatoes
1/2 cup	brandy
1 cup	lobster stock
1 1/3 cup	heavy cream
salt and pepper to taste	
1 lb.	cooked fusilli pasta

For the lobster:
- Heat oil in a sauté pan over a high flame.
- Sauté the lobster tails in olive oil for 1-2 minutes.
- Add the shallots, peas, lobster meat, sun-dried tomatoes and sauté for another 2 minutes. Keep stirring the ingredients the entire time you are cooking this dish.
- Add the brandy and burn off, approximately 1 minute.
- Stir in the cream and lobster stock and simmer until suitable thickness is achieved, approximately 3-4 minutes.
- Season with salt and pepper to taste.

To complete:
- Add the cooked pasta, toss, and serve.

Wine pairing:
- Pinot Grigio, California Montini

MON AMI GABI
Paris Las Vegas

Claude Gaty

Some chefs feel a calling to their work. Paris-born Claude Gaty, a gentle giant of a man with a slight French accent and humble smile, is definitely one of them. "I knew, as I shadowed my grandmother in the kitchen when I was a child, that I was where I was supposed to be," he says. "From a very early age, and when most boys were playing soccer, I was picking fresh fruits and vegetables."

Gaty was raised by his Alsacian grandmother, whose work in aristocratic households in France included an apprenticeship in the Rothschild Chateau. "She was my teacher and I was exposed to fine food through her," says Gaty. That exposure grew to become the passion of his adulthood.

But it was when he began training in kitchens in the United States in 1977, then opened his own restaurant, La Bretagne, in Maui, Hawaii, that Gaty learned to meld his heritage of regional French cooking with a contemporary flair. Leaving the tropics for Chicago, he opened Bistro Zinc with Rene Bajeux, bringing French bistro cooking to the Windy City. Now, as chef partner of Mon Ami Gabi restaurant at Paris Las Vegas (there are four of them across the country), he calls his current cuisine "contemporary French bistro."

His favorite ingredients are extra virgin olive oil, fresh herbs, and balsamic vinegar, and his favorite dishes are a simple roasted chicken and, in winter, braised short ribs. In addition to roast duck, lamb stew, and a host of other popular bistro fare, Gaty serves traditional French staples, such as crepes, quiches, and pommes frites—those wide crispy-fried potatoes beloved by Parisians who sit and watch the world pass by their sidewalk tables. "It's always a challenge to keep the menu exciting, with daily specials of the season," he says. "When vendors offer me something new, I always take them

up on it, so I can present something a little different."

An oh-so-French whole crusty baguette arrives at each table in a white paper bag. "I would love to ask Dr. Atkins, father of the low-carb diet, whatever happened to the concept of everything in moderation?" says Gaty. "To me it doesn't get any better than a crusty loaf of bread, some cheese, and a glass of wine."

To get his culinary creative juices flowing, Gaty says he likes to travel and eat out. "I love going to different farmers markets, and specialty and gourmet shops, especially when I am visiting different cities."

In addition to providing simple food and good wine, Gaty's goal is to make people happy as they dine. "I want to make sure everyone is smiling, laughing, and having a good time," he says. "I enjoy life and serving others."

Mon Ami Gabi, which means "my friend Gabi," is named after its founder: Chef Gabino Sotelino. "Gabi entrusted me with the task of keeping the world of true French dining and lifestyle in this magnificent city." It's French as the French would know it—casual with plenty of old-world atmosphere, including white small-tile floors, dark mahogany woodwork, European-style arches trimmed with glass, red-velvet draperies, stained glass, and fin-de-siècle chandeliers. Terrace dining includes the required sidewalk café, one of the few on the Las Vegas Strip, which offers a view of the dancing waters across the street at Bellagio. Close your eyes and you're sitting on the Champs Elysée, missing only the smell of French cigarettes and the guttural accents at the next table. "The brasserie style and open-air dining on the patio is a wonderful addition to the traditional closed-in eating venues Americans typically visit," says Gaty. "It's a nice complement of environment and food."

Skate with Capers

brown butter and haricots verts salad

Serves 4

Skate

4	skate wings, cleaned
1/2 cup	flour
6 oz.	vegetable oil, for cooking
2 oz.	capers
4 pinch	chopped parsley
2 medium	lemons, juiced
2 oz.	brown butter
salt and pepper to taste	
vegetable salad, distributed equally	

Skate vegetable salad

1 large	red tomato, seeded and julienne with skin on
1/4	red onion, julienne
1 medium	fennel bulb, julienne
1/2 lb.	haricots verts
1 pinch	chopped parsley

Vinaigrette

1 tbsp.	champagne vinegar
3 tbsp.	extra virgin olive oil
salt and pepper to taste	

For brown butter:
• Melt 2 ounces of unsalted butter until dark brown to obtain a nutty taste. Discard the solids.

For the haricots verts salad:
• Cook the haricots verts in boiling water and salt until al dente.
• Shock the haricots verts in ice water, then drain.
• Add the vegetables to the bowl and toss.
• Add the vinaigrette.

For the vinaigrette:
• Whisk vinegar, oil, and seasonings together.

For the skate:
• Season the skate wings with salt and pepper. Coat lightly with flour and shake off excess.
• Warm oil in a non-stick pan and sear skate on each side for 2 minutes (total of 4 minutes) until golden in color.
• With a fish spatula, place skate delicately on the plate, being careful not to split it.
• Drain oil from the pan. Add the capers. Deglaze with lemon juice. Add the melted brown butter and chopped parsley.

To complete the entrée:
• Place the skate on warm plates.
• Swirl the pan around and pour the sauce over the fish.
• Place the vegetable salad on the plate next to the skate and serve.

Wine pairing:
• Meursault, Louis Jadot 1999

Steak Frites

Serves 4

Steak

4 10-oz.	prime, centercut, aged, top sirloin butt steaks
1 bunch	watercress, for garnish
4 ea.	disks of Classic butter
1 tbsp.	chopped garlic (optional)
1/4 cup	extra virgin olive oil

salt and cracked black pepper to taste

Classic butter

1/4 bunch	parsley, stems removed
1/2 lb.	unsalted butter
1 tbsp.	Dijon mustard
1 tsp.	chopped fresh tarragon leaves
1 tbsp.	lemon juice
1 pinch	ground black pepper
1 pinch	salt
1 medium	shallot, chopped

Fries or Frites

6 ea.	70 count Idaho Russet Burbank potatoes, peeled

salt to taste
vegetable oil for frying potatoes

For the steak:
- Pound the steaks to tenderize, to 1/2" thickness.
- Four hours prior to cooking, brush steaks with olive oil and sprinkle with the cracked black pepper and garlic. Refrigerate.

For the classic butter:
- Combine all the ingredients in a food processor and mix to a fine paste.
- Transfer butter to a sheet of wax paper and roll to form a cylinder. Refrigerate. When firm, slice into 1/4" disks.

For cooking the fries or frites:
- Slice into 1/4" width with a French mandoline.
- Place the potato slices in cold water to wash off excess starch. Remove from water and pat dry with paper towels.
- Cook the fries in oil heated to 340°. Cook until crisp, but without color.
- Remove from the oil and place on a sheet pan to cool.
- To serve, fry in 375° oil until light brown in color.
- Shake off excess oil and salt to taste.

To complete the entrée:
- Sprinkle salt on both sides of steaks and grill to the desired temperature.
- Remove from grill and place on plates.
- Top steaks with one disk of classic butter.
- Serve fries piled beside steaks.
- Garnish plates with fresh watercress and serve.

Wine pairing:
- Gigondas, E. Guigal, 2000

Barry S. Dakake

It's trendy, sleek, chic. Chic: ultra-suede and hide-skin banquettes, dark wood tables with brushed aluminum accents, and mosaic mirrored columns that reflect like glittering disco balls. Trendy: limestone walls and a center champagne-and-caviar bar with snazzy little stools and a glowing bar rail for the bar flies. Sleek: a glass-enclosed wine cellar and a two-sided waterfall.

But the coolest effect is the domed ceiling, covered in silver leaf, programmed with a 300-color lighting system to bathe the action below in changing hues. Wow.

Chef Barry S. Dakake (pronounced Day-cake) adds his own wow to this Las Vegas sister of the original N9NE Steakhouse, which debuted in Chicago in 2000. Born in Rhode Island, his star began to rise in New York City, where he worked with Charlie Palmer and Neil Murphy for six years at the Four Seasons and Aureole. He's no "just-grill-the-steak" kind of chef. "I always want to do something new and be the best at it," says Dakake.

Fresh ingredients, of course, are number one for creating a tasty healthy meal. Dakake is lucky to have a culinary heritage to draw upon. "I'm half Italian, half Syrian," he explains. "Growing up we had wonderful meals of fresh foods and ethnic flavors."

He trained in the culinary program at the Rhode Island School of Design. "I graduated with a class of eighteen," he says. "The personalization, intensity, and ability to work closely with top chefs were incredible. You either had the heart for culinary or you were out. There was great pressure to be the best. I credit Chef Leon Dhanens for bringing out the chef in me."

Dakake gets turned on by sharing his knowledge. "I love to teach and to tell," he says. "To be a great chef, you have to be able to translate the information to your team. You're nothing without a great team behind you. I couldn't do this without my team—they're part of my family."

Dakake's favorite dish is a slow-roast barbecue and his favorite herb is fresh basil. For those who want to venture beyond the excellent aged steaks, his menu includes contemporary American cuisine—inventive seafood appetizers such as "Two Cones," featuring Asian tuna tartare and a citrus Maine lobster salad or oysters Rockefeller with spinach and parmesan cheese. Entrees include such interesting combinations as roasted Colorado lamb chops in a parmesan crust with rosemary jus, or an organic truffle chicken with roasted potatoes, garlic, fennel, and white truffle oil. And let's not forget the side dish of lobster mashed potatoes.

Barry's goal is to be known for delivering a relaxing dining experience, which includes superb food, excellent service, and great atmosphere. He seems to have achieved it at N9NE. "I love it when the guests ask to meet the chef, or come back into the kitchen, he says. "When a diner tells us that we've exceeded their expectations, that is the greatest compliment." But what's really cool, he confesses, "is when Hollywood celebrities call ahead to ask us to prepare their favorite meal and deliver it to their suite—sometimes in another hotel!"

Dakake's one wish is that his grandfather could see him now. "Poppa loved good food," he says. "I would love to tell him, 'Look Poppa, I finally made it!'"

Roasted Chicken

with Red Bliss potatoes and white truffles

Serves 4

4 large	whole chicken breasts (from a 5-lb. chicken)
4 large	Red Bliss potatoes
4 bulbs	garlic
4 medium	red onions
1-1/2 cups	chicken stock
1 cup	whole butter
20 oz.	white truffle oil
3	fresh summer truffles, shaved

For the chicken:
- Preheat oven to 375°.
- Season the chicken breasts with salt and pepper.
- Lightly oil a hot sauté pan and place chicken in, skin side down.
- Cut the potato and onion into quarters and trim off the bottom half of the garlic so it sits flat.
- Add the vegetables to the pan with the chicken and place in the oven for 25 minutes. Remove pan from oven. Take chicken out of the pan, place in a warm area, and allow to rest while you finish the sauce.
- Drain off any excess grease and add the chicken stock. Reduce by half.
- Add butter and whisk until thickened.
- Season with salt and pepper.

To serve:
- Place on warm plates. Pour sauce over the chicken. Drizzle truffle oil around the dish.
- Top with fresh shaved truffle.

Wine pairing:
- 1999 Chambolle-Musgny, Lignier-Michelot

Chef Barry S. Dakake © 2005 N9NE Steakhouse

Bone-In Ribeye

with lobster mashed potatoes

Serves 4

Bone-in ribeye

4 8-oz.   bone-in ribeyes (prime)
1 cup   veal reduction
salt and fresh ground pepper

Lobster mashed potatoes

5 lbs.   whole Yukon Gold potatoes
1-1/2 lbs.   whole butter
1 quart   heavy cream
1 quart   lobster or fish stock
1 lb.   lobster meat, cooked and
              chopped
salt and white pepper

For the potatoes:
• Peel potatoes. Boil the whole potatoes in heavily salted water.
• Heat the heavy cream in a sauce pan.
• In a separate sauce pan, reduce the lobster stock by half.
• When the potatoes are fork tender, add the butter and place through a food mill into a large mixing bowl.
• Add the cream and season with salt and white pepper.
• Once the lobster stock is reduced, add the lobster meat to the reduction.
• Fold half of the lobster-meat reduction mix into the potatoes and save the other half to pour over the top.

For the ribeye:
• Preheat the grill to very hot.
• Season the ribeye generously with salt and fresh ground black pepper.
• Grill for 8 minutes on each side to reach a nice medium-rare to medium.

To complete the entrée:
• Place the steak on the plate and pour the hot veal reduction over the top of the steak.
• Place the potatoes on the side of the plate and serve.

Wine pairing:
• 1999 Reynolds Family, Stag's Leap Reserve, Napa Cabernet Sauvignon

NINE FINE IRISHMEN
New York-New York

Kevin Dundon

Exports from Irish pubs may be more famous than those from an Irish kitchen, but Kevin Dundon, executive chef of Nine Fine Irishmen, proves that Irish food should enjoy the celebrity status of Guiness and Stout. "We want to smash up the preconceptions Americans have about Irish food," he says to explain his concept of a menu that goes far beyond what Americans may know of Irish specialties. "Instead of using a lot of sauces and marinades, we focus on buying the highest quality meats and authentic natural ingredients and serving them with a twist."

High-quality for this Irish farm boy means fresh fresh fresh, grown organically, and flown in from Ireland. "I love the idea of picking the fruit and veggies right from the garden that will become the evening meal," he says. When faced with restrictions on importing Irish pork sausage to the U.S., Dundon imported his butcher, instead, who advised the local vendors on sausage quality, texture, and flavor.

Trained in Dublin, Dundon moved on to kitchens in Switzerland and Canada before returning to his homeland. There, on the southeast coast, he and his wife, Catherine, are the proprietors of the award-winning Dunbrody Country House Hotel & Restaurant. Monthly flights to Las Vegas keep him in tune with the U.S. kitchen. He revises the menu during each visit and between times he communicates with the chefs in America via Web Cam.

Dundon calls his cuisine Modern Contemporary—a blend of his deep roots in the Emerald Isle and his international experience. You won't find corned beef and cabbage on the menu here. "I'm raising the idea of pub grub to a new level, tweaking traditional Irish recipes," he says. The healthy new cuisine has enchanted such celebrities as U2, Brad Pitt, Julia Roberts, and even the Queen of England.

The pub is a natural venue for Dundon; the ritual of dining with friends and family is something he has cherished since childhood. "My grandfather was the rock of my life," he says. "He lived for his food and eating with the family. The occasion of eating together is a social relationship and the pub has always been a social gathering point." Dundon turns wistful: "I wish my grandfather could see me today."

No doubt his grandfather would be impressed with Nine Fine Irishmen at the spectacular New York-New York. It's about as close to authentic as it gets. The two-level pub is literally a bit of the Old Sod—built and shipped in nine packed containers from Ireland. Quaint may be an understatement for the vast collection of Irish memorabilia that fills the ornate Victorian bar and the intimate nooks and "snugs"—couples-only hideaways named from the days when women were not allowed to imbibe in public. Oscar Wilde's quip, "Resist everything but temptation," inscribed into the floor, is an invitation for patrons to let loose. Festive Irish music and, of course, stouts, lagers, and creamy ales add to the fun.

But who are those nine fine namesakes? They were Irishmen of varying backgrounds and temperaments, all idealistic members of the Young Ireland Movement in 1848, inspired by the romantic notions of nationalism that were swirling throughout Europe at the time. Although proponents of peaceful reform, they were captured and convicted of treason by Her Majesty's government. Seven were deported to Australia. It's their very notion of Irishness that is celebrated in this Las Vegas pub.

Loin of Bacon

with an Irish Mist glaze served on a potato cake

Serves 4

2 lbs.	loin of bacon or pork loin
16	cloves
1 dash	Irish Mist or whiskey (add 1 tsp. honey)
1/4 cup	clear honey
1 cup	apple cider
1/2 cup	leeks
3 tbsp.	butter
1 lb.	cooked and mashed potatoes
3 tbsp.	flour
1/4 cup	cream
1	egg yolk
8	cherry tomatoes (cut into 4 sections)
3/4 cup	sliced leeks

For the loin:
- Preheat the oven to 220°.
- Steam the bacon for 45 minutes, then allow to cool.
- Cut into 4 x 4 cm slices and insert the cloves through the skin of each bacon slice. Place the bacon in a roasting pan and brush with the honey and Irish Mist.
- Cook in the oven for 10-15 minutes until the honey caramelizes; remove from the oven and set the bacon aside to rest while you make the sauce.
- Put the roasting pan on the top of the stove, over a high heat; add the apple cider and reduce by half.

For the potato cakes and to complete the entrée:
- Chop the reserved bacon and the dark green part of the leeks and sauté in a little butter.
- Add this mixture to the mashed potato with the flour, cream, and egg yolk, then mold into small round discs.
- Pan fry for 2 minutes on each side, then place in the oven for another 2 minutes.
- Fry the white part of the leeks and cherry tomatoes with some butter for 3 minutes until soft, then season to taste.
- Place a potato cake on the plate with the leek and cherry tomatoes. Slice the bacon over the top and drizzle the sauce around the plate.

Wine pairing:
- Vin de Pays d'Oc Shiraz Chantovent

Dunbrody Kiss

Serves 4

Dunbrody chocolate kiss

5 large	egg yolks
1 lb.	dark chocolate
2 cups	heavy cream
5 large	egg whites, beaten to a peak
1 regular	Mars Bar
2 oz.	corn flakes
1/4 cup	chocolate ganache

Ganache

8 ounces	high-quality semi-sweet chocolate, chopped
1 cup	heavy cream
2 tbsp.	unsalted butter

For the ganache:
- Place the chocolate in large bowl.
- Heat the cream and butter in a saucepan over medium heat until hot, but not boiling.
- Pour the hot cream over the chocolate and stir until the chocolate is melted and smooth.

For the finishing of the Dunbrody Kiss:
- Whisk the egg yolks until light in color and thick.
- Melt the chocolate and add the whipped egg yolk.
- Whip the cream to a soft peak and whisk into the chocolate and egg mixture.
- Fold in the beaten egg whites and refrigerate until serving time.
- Melt the Mars Bar and stir in the corn flakes for a crispy base.
- In an individual mold, 3" round x 2" tall, place the crispy candy base on the bottom and top with the chocolate mousse. Place in the fridge for about 4 hours.
- Place the chilled and firm Kisses on a rack. Unmold the Kisses. Pour the liquid ganache evenly over the Kisses.
- Refrigerate until serving.
- Serve with a drizzle of chocolate sauce.

Cindy Hutson

"I never wanted to be a chef," says Cindy Hutson, who, as fate would have it, currently owns five thriving restaurants. She and her now ex-husband were busy importing Jamaican products to the U.S. when her life changed. "In the throes of an amicable divorce, I realized I needed to do something to support myself and my two children," she says.

But the story really starts when she was growing up with a mother who hated to cook. "From the time I was nine years old, I would watch the 'Galloping Gourmet' and 'Chef Tell' and write down the ingredients for my mom to buy at the grocery," recalls Hutson. "Then I would cook away to my heart's content. It was a survival technique to keep from eating Twinkies and frozen veggies. It turned into a passion."

With the urgent need to make a living, passion became practicality. She and her partner, Delius, whose mother was a successful restaurateur, opened a 45-seat restaurant on South Beach in Miami. "We literally built it from scratch—painting, making the tables, picking the fabric and upholstering the chairs," says Hutson. When they were finished, Hutson asked who the chef would be. Delius looked at her. "You," he said.

With no formal training or technique, Hutson took up the challenge. "I donned a summer dress and apron and we opened," she says. It wasn't all that easy. "Every night I burned and cut myself," she confesses. "I cried every night behind that stove."

But after four months, the first review was glowing. "They called the restaurant a 'jewel of the sun' and said the food was exceptional," says Hutson. "I stopped crying and said, 'OK, maybe I am doing this right.'"

Her food has been described as melding the flavors of South America, Asia, and the West Indies. Hutson says it's an eclectic combination from her life and has dubbed it "Cuisine of the Sun." Think warm tropical breezes, the lilting rhythms of the Caribbean, and fresh interesting combinations of ingredients. "My food reflects the wonderful flavors of the places where I've lived and traveled," explains Hutson. "My travels have enabled me to open up the menu and expand the palate."

She grew up in New Jersey and New England "where chowders are wonderful." But family roots are in the Deep South. "Five generations of ancestors are from Mobile, Alabama," she says. "We would visit the family homestead, where I would sit on the porch and just feel the history, the spirit. That comes out in my recipes that include black-eyed peas and bouillabaisses and lots of greens." She lives in Florida now, where there's lots of fresh seafood. And, of course, the Jamaican connection is strong. "People think of me as a Jamaican-style cook," she says. "But the title 'Cuisine of the Sun' really means healthy and fun."

For Hutson, food and ambience are inseparable. "I have an ability to take these wonderful combinations of ingredients and balance them with the five senses," she says. "I can't explain why or how I have this talent, but it works incredibly well. All my restaurants are in soft muted tones that make you feel warm. I want to know that I have delivered a full dining experience that uses all five senses. If my guests come away totally satisfied, I have done a good job and at the end of the day I'm happy."

Jerk Double Pork Chop

with guava-spiced rum sauce

Serves 6

Guava-spiced rum sauce

4 tbsp.	unsalted butter
3 large	yellow onions, sliced
1-1/2 cups	spiced rum
2 jars	guava jelly, 10 oz.
3 cups	water
1/2 cup	Busha Browne Planters Sauce (imported Jamaican sauce)

Jerk paste

1 large	onion, minced
2 tbsp.	fresh thyme leaves
1 bunch	scallions, chopped
4 cloves	garlic, crushed
1/2 cup	parsley
2 large	Scotch bonnet peppers, seeded and chopped
1 tsp.	fresh ground black pepper
1/4 cup	fresh ground Jamaican allspice
1/4 tsp.	grated nutmeg
1 tsp.	cinnamon
1 tbsp.	kosher salt
1/4 cup	teriyaki sauce
1/4 cup	soy sauce

Pork chops in jerk marinade

6 16-oz.	center-cut pork chops with two ribs
3 tbsp.	jerk paste
2 cloves	garlic, chopped
1 cup	teriyaki sauce
1/4 cup	sesame oil
1 tbsp.	mushroom soy sauce
2 tbsp.	kosher salt
	unsalted butter

Jasmine rice

1 cup	white rice
2-1/4 cups	water
3 sprigs	thyme
1 scotch	bonnet or havanero pepper
1 tbsp.	butter

For the guava-spiced rum sauce:

• In an 8-quart saucepan, cook the onions and butter until caramelized golden brown. Add the rum and simmer for 4-5 minutes.
• Add the guava jelly and water. Stir until the jelly is melted. Add the Busha Browne Planters Sauce and remove from heat.
• Purée the hot sauce in a blender until smooth. Add a little water if the sauce is too thick.

For the jerk paste:

• Place all the ingredients in a food processor and blend, drizzling in the teriyaki and soy sauce to make a smooth paste. Store in the refrigerator.

For the jerk marinade:

• Whisk together the garlic, teriyaki sauce, sesame oil, and mushroom soy sauce.

For the pork chops:

• In a mixing bowl combine the jerk paste and pork chops with the jerk marinade and refrigerate from 3 hours to overnight.

To complete:

• Sear the pork chops in a hot sauté pan until browned. Place in a preheated 425° oven for 18 minutes or until the pork chops are cooked to medium or 135° internal temperature.
• Place the pork chops in the center of 6 warm plates. Drizzle with the guava-spiced rum sauce.
• Serve with the jasmine rice and your favorite vegetable.

Wine pairing:

• Martinelli Zinfandel, Guiseppe and Luisa or Penfolds St. Henri Shiraz

Ortanique Venison

with sauce

Serves 4

Venison

2 whole	venison racks, 8 ribs each (New Zealand Cervena preferred)
1/4 cup	olive oil

Marinade

4 cloves	garlic, crushed
1/4 cup	Dijon mustard
1/4 cup	tomato paste
1/4 cup	Worcestershire sauce
1/4 cup	olive oil
1 tbsp.	kosher salt
1 tbsp.	fresh cracked pepper

Venison sauce

4-6	shallots, sliced
4 cloves	garlic, smashed and chopped
2 tbsp.	butter, salted
2 each	rosemary sprigs
1/2 cup	ginger, dried, candied, diced
3/4 cup	sour cherries, dried
1/2 cup	brandy
2 quart	veal stock

For the venison sauce:
- Soak the cherries and ginger in the brandy for several hours. Set aside at room temperature for later use.
- Slowly sauté the shallots and garlic in a saucepan with salted butter until they're nicely caramelized.
- Take care not to burn. When shallots and garlic are browned, pull from the stove and add the cherry-ginger brandy.
- **Be careful: the brandy might ignite.** Put back on the stove to burn off the alcohol.
- Add the veal stock and bring to a boil. When it has reached a boil, turn down to a simmer and reduce by half.
- Strain the sauce through a fine chinoise. It should have a syrupy consistency. Add salt and pepper to taste.

For the marinade:
- Blend the ingredients for the marinade until it reaches a paste-like consistency.

For the venison racks:
- French the chops by using a sharp knife to cut the fat and meat from the ribs. Do not cut into the tenderloin. Set aside the trimmed meat.
- Rub the marinade all over the racks and set aside at least 1 hour or in the refrigerator overnight.
- In a hot sauté pan with the olive oil, sear the venison racks about 4 minutes on each side. Put the venison on a wire rack in a shallow roasting pan and place in a preheated 400° oven. Using a meat thermometer, roast until the internal temperature reaches 130° or mid-rare.
- Remove the venison racks from the oven and let rest for 5 minutes before cutting into the single chops.

To complete:
- Serve 2 chops per plate and spoon the heated sauce over the chops (about 2 ounces for each plate).
- Serve with mashed potatoes and sautéed vegetables.

Wine pairing:
- Shafer Relentless Syrah
- Malbec, Bramare from Argentina

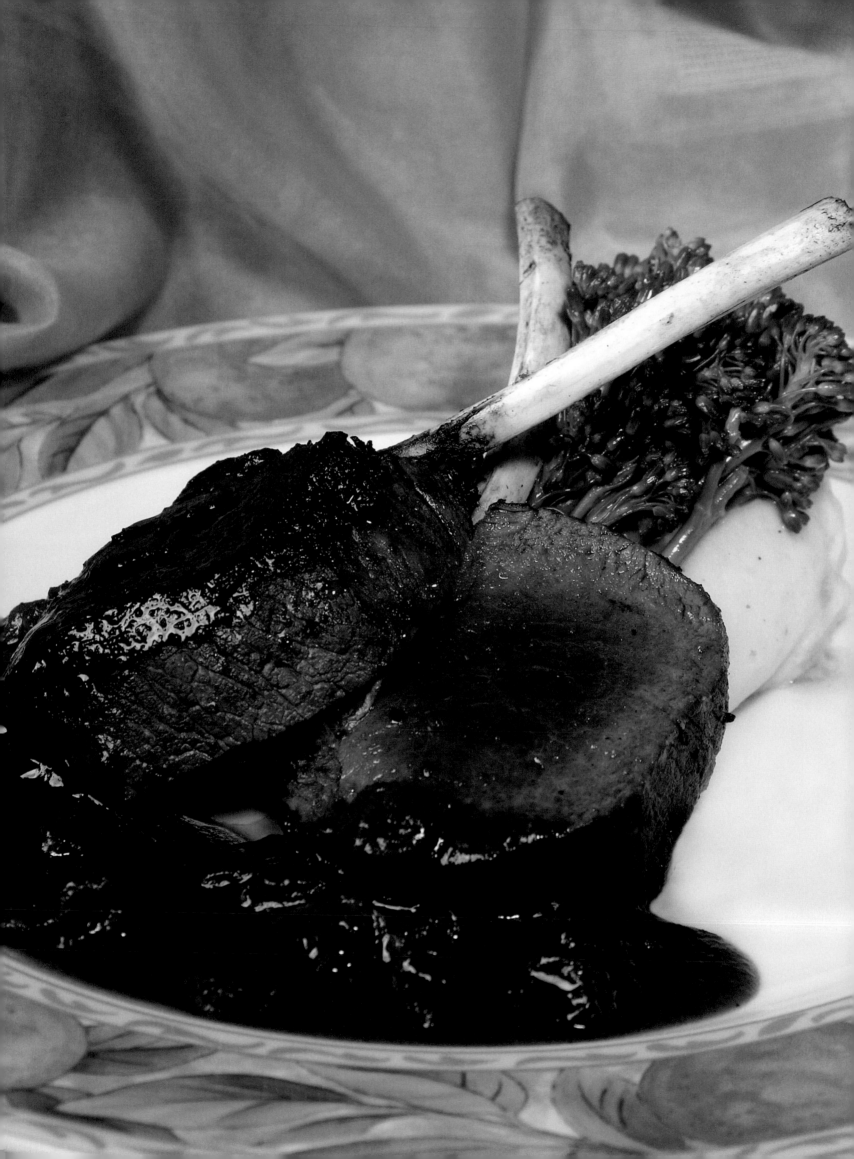

OSTERIA DEL CIRCO
Bellagio

James Benson

*2004 Award of Excellence,
Wine Spectator*

Unlike many celebrity chefs who are born abroad and come to the U.S. to find their fortunes in American kitchens, James Benson is a home-grown boy from the San Francisco Bay Area. He went to college to study engineering.

But something happened along the way. "My family was in the food-processing and manufacturing business and I grew up with big family meals," he says. "I remember baking with my mom at a very young age. She's Italian and we had a very multicultural upbringing. Foods from all ethnic regions appeared on our table. That strong culinary influence became a passion as I grew older. Food was the center of it all."

Along the way, he foresake engineering for kitchen duty in the culinary arts program at San Francisco City College. There he flourished, graduating with honors, and he soon landed a job at the prestigious oliveto in Oakland. "Michael Tusk and Christopher Fernandez at oliveto were important influences on my development as a chef," says Benson. "They instilled in me the ideas of hard work and creativity."

Inspired by the possibilities of Italian cuisine, Benson set out to apprentice in Italy. It wasn't hard for a man of his talents to join a one-star Michelin restaurant. From there he worked his way along the Italian Riviera. At the two-star restaurant, Balzi Rossi, he was recruited by restaurateur Mario Maccioni to return to the U.S. to cook at the famous Le Cirque 2000 in New York. He worked under the acclaimed Sottha Khuhn and Marc Poidevin. He later would join Poidevin in Las Vegas.

That history took him to Las Vegas as executive sous chef of Le Cirque and its lighter-hearted Italian cousin,

Osteria del Circo, both at Bellagio. There he worked with Poidevin and Enzo Secci. "Enzo's love for Tuscan cuisine pushed me to approach it in a new and innovative light," says Benson. "His commitment inspired me to do my very best."

As chef de cuisine at Osteria del Circo, Benson creates what he calls "simple" cuisine. "It's my desire to introduce new ideas and tastes without surprise or exaggeration," he says. "I want to bring the guest a meal that is both elegant and sophisticated. That's why I love working with seasonal produce. We change the menu four to five times a year, which allows us the opportunity to be creative, while offering a unique experience." Some of his favorite foods are rabbit, wild boar with pasta, and wild mushrooms. "I can cook rabbit several ways," he says.

He often strolls through the farmers' market in San Francisco to let his mind explore the possibilities in the produce he finds there. Benson uses products that are as organic as possible: hormone-free beef, wild fish, free-roaming chickens. "Yes, you can taste the difference between these types of products and those found in the local supermarket," he says.

"I want to bring the natural quality and flavors of the food out in a simple plate." He returns to Italy every year to absorb wisdom from the great Italian chefs.

Benson's award-winning food is served in the whimsical atmosphere of the Osterio del Circo, or circus tavern. Meant to resemble a 19th century European circus, the décor is festive and bold. Bright reds and yellows billow in tenting on the ceiling. Playful sculptures in circus themes accent luxurious fabrics, creating a comfortable light-hearted environment.

Snapper in Cartoccio

Hawaiian shrimp, braised fennel, cherry tomatoes, and capers

Serves 4

Snapper

4 pieces	aluminum foil measuring 18" x 18"
4 bulbs	fennel, sliced and sautéed in olive oil fennel fronds
1 pkg.	small basket of cherry or grape tomatoes
6 medium	Fingerling potatoes, peeled, cut in half lengthwise, boiled
4 tsp.	fresh capers
4 cups	fish stock
4 6-oz.	boneless filets of tai snapper
8 large	head-on shrimp (15 count)
4 oz.	extra virgin olive oil
salt and pepper	

For the snapper:

- On a large flat surface, place an oval beveled plate.
- Place one sheet of foil at a time on top of the plate so that half of the foil is resting on top of the plate and the other half is hanging off. Push the foil down into the plate so that it forms a slight bowl effect.
- In the center of the 'bowl' place 1/4 of the sautéed fennel. (We like to sauté the fennel in extra virgin olive oil. Our procedure is to heat the olive oil in a medium-sized sauté pan, add a filet of salted chopped anchovy, one clove of chopped garlic, a pinch of crushed red pepper, and a bit of chopped fennel fronds, then let them sweat until the garlic turns translucent. At this time we add our fennel, season with salt and pepper, and cook over a low flame until tender.)
- Arrange 1/4 of the basket of the cherry tomatoes, three halves of the fingerling potatoes, and 1 teaspoon of capers. Around the fennel, compose all of the ingredients neatly in the base of the 'bowl' and add 1 cup of seasoned fish stock.
- Place one filet of a tai snapper and 2 shrimp; season with salt and pepper and a drizzle of extra virgin olive oil.
- Place the filet on the top of the vegetable base, top with the two shrimp and a fennel frond, and drizzle with extra virgin olive oil.
- Seal the bag by folding the foil in half so the corners meet and the closed side is toward you. Take the far edge and make your first fold about 1" thick; repeat on the sides so that you form an envelope. Make about 3-4 folds so that you end up with an airtight envelope measuring roughly 6" in width by 9" in length. Repeat the process for the other 3 filets. You should now have 4 nice envelopes, which in Italian translates as *cartoccio*.
- Preheat your oven to 425°, lay the *cartoccio* on a sheet pan and place it in the preheated oven. The cooking process is approximately 8-10 minutes. When you take the *cartoccio* out of the oven, it will have blown up like a balloon.

To complete:

- In the restaurant, the snapper is presented in the envelope to our guests. We open the envelope in front of them: It creates excitement and releases incredible aromas.
- You can either serve directly in the *cartoccio* or portion it for your guests.

Wine pairing:

- Vermentino from Liguria or Sardegnia or Veranaccia from Tuscany.

Loin of Rabbit

wrapped in pancetta, polenta timbale, braised leg, roasted rack

Serves 4

Rabbit
2 1-lb.	rabbits, whole, dressed
1/2 tsp.	thyme, freshly chopped
1/2 tsp.	rosemary, freshly chopped
1/4 tsp.	sage, freshly chopped
12	pancetta, 12" long strips, cut no thicker than 1/16"
salt and pepper	

Stock for the braise
Rabbit bones and front legs cut into 1" lengths	
1 medium	onion
1 small	carrot
1 branch	celery
3 sprigs	thyme
1/4 cup	white wine
1/2 gallon	chicken stock

Braising the rabbit legs
4	rabbit hind legs
1/4 cup	olive oil
1/2 tsp.	thyme, freshly chopped
1/2 tsp.	rosemary, freshly chopped
1/4 tsp.	sage, freshly chopped
1	bay leaf
1/4 cup	carrot, diced at 1/4"
1/4 cup	leek, diced at 1/4"
1/4 cup	celery, diced at 1/4"
1 cup	red onion, diced at 1/4"
2 cloves	garlic, chopped
1 tbsp.	tomato paste
1 cup	dry white wine
1 oz.	porcini, dried
salt and pepper	

Polenta timbale
1/2 cup	polenta bramata
2 cups	salted water
2 tbsp.	mascarpone cheese
1 tbsp.	extra virgin olive oil

Preparing the rabbit:
• To dress the rabbits, take a boning knife and remove the front and hind legs. Now that the legs have been removed, take a cleaver and make your first cut at the tail end where the loin hits the h-bone. Save the bones, as you will need them for the stock.
• Now take the cleaver and cut though the second to last bone of the rack to divide the rack from the saddle.
• With a pair of scissors, cut at about 1/2" across the tops of the rack so that the inner cage is visible. Split the racks off the spine and scrape the back of the rib cage so that you can peel off the cap. You should now have two frenched rabbit racks.
• Moving on to the saddle, lay the rabbit saddle flat on a cutting board with the flaps spread open. With a boning knife, start parallel to the spine. Push the knife gently against the bone and push outwards from the spine. Leave the tenderloin attached. Change the direction of your knife and cut back under the bones toward the spine, then slide the knife down toward the board to remove the loin. Repeat the process with the other loins.
• Now that you have your boneless rabbit loins, open them up flat, season with salt and pepper, sprinkles of freshly chopped rosemary, thyme, and sage, and roll the flap over the loin. Take your pancetta strips and stretch them out onto a flat surface. Place the loin on top of the strip, rolling the pancetta around the loin as you roll the rabbit loin. Refrigerate until use.

Preparing the stock for the braise:
• In a sauce pot, heat 2 teaspoons of olive oil and sear bones and front legs until golden brown.
• Deglaze with white wine, add in vegetables (roughly cut), and cover with the chicken stock. Let cook for two hours over a low flame.
• Strain and reserve the stock for the braised rabbit legs.

For the rabbit legs:
• In a large sauce pan, heat up a couple of tablespoons of olive oil. Season the legs with the chopped herbs, salt, and pepper. Sear the legs in the hot oil, remove, and add in your diced vegetables. Lower the flame and cook the vegetables until tender.
• Add your seared rabbit legs back into the pan, add in 1 ounce of dried porcini mushrooms, 1 tablespoon of tomato paste, 1 cup of dry white wine, and a bay leaf, then cover with the rabbit stock.
• Cook over a low flame for 1-1/2 hours until the meat becomes tender and is easily pulled away from the bone.

For the polenta timbale:

- Bring your water to a simmer.
- Whisk polenta in a thin stream and let simmer on a low flame for about an hour, stirring periodically so that the polenta does not stick or form a crust.
- Pull off of fire and add mascarpone and olive oil. Let cool for 15 minutes.
- Take four 4-oz. soufflé cups and pour polenta into them. Chill.

To complete:

- Sear the wrapped rabbit loins in a sauté pan until golden brown.
- Add in your racks and place into a 375° oven, rotating after 3-4 minutes. Cook for a total of 8-10 minutes.
- Remove from pan and let rest.
- Place your preheated polenta timbale off center on a plate.
- Lean a braised rabbit leg next to the timbale, slice the loin into 1/4" slices, and fan the loin onto the plate.
- Garnish with the roasted rack and a bouquet of fresh herbs, then finish with some of the strained and reduced braising juice.

Wine pairing:

- Trentino or Friulli or a Sangiovese Varietal

Julian Serrano

2004 Grand Award, Wine Spectator

More than $60 million worth of original paintings, ceramics, tiles, and sculptures by Pablo Picasso surround you in this elegant Mediterranean dining room. They may take your mind off the meal that arrives at your table—but only for a moment. Julian Serrano's creations from the kitchen are every bit as much works of art as those of the restaurant's namesake.

Serrano was already a star when he came to Bellagio in Las Vegas. He'd received the James Beard Regional Award for Best Chef in California for Masa's restaurant in San Francisco. It was quite a feat for the farm boy who left his native Spain at 15 and chose cooking as a way to finance his yen for travel. "I knew that travel required money, and I did not speak many languages," says Serrano. "Cooking had no language barriers, so I learned to cook and I traveled throughout Europe working in kitchens." Along the way he learned to speak English, Italian, and French.

Whatever language he speaks in the kitchen, it has made him loved by his staff. Not for Serrano the temper tantrums of the egocentric kitchen master. He's humble and warm. "The ego cannot get in the way of the food," he says. "The chef is not alone, it's the team. Your staff must respect you—you are their leader. They look to you for guidance, education, and understanding. When you work beside them, you build a strong team that is focused. Together each of us becomes a better person."

Quality ingredients are the foundation of Serrano's food. "I look for new ingredients each season," he says. "I speak to my suppliers at midnight, placing the order for the freshest product coming from the market or farmer. The products from abroad are purchased and FedEx'd the same day."

But fresh isn't the only criterion for excellence. "How the product is raised, handled, or shipped is important to the quality," he explains. "If it's meat, I want to know what the animal was fed. If it's produce, what type of earth—how is it treated or touched in what manner? I want to know where the fish came from."

Although Serrano is Spanish, he calls his cooking French Mediterranean. His favorite ingredients are tomatoes, olive oil, vinegars, and fish. "It's really not a movement," he says. "It's my own creativity with the background of knowledge I have and with the choice of ingredients I work with. Like the artist, I am not limited by materials or imagination."

Serrano fuels all that creativity by playing tennis and bicycling. "Exercise is important to maintain my energy level," he says. "From 6 pm until midnight, I am nonstop—moving, yelling, running the more than 26 kitchen employees and greeting guests in the front of the house. I must have high energy to create the intensity and flow we need to handle the volume and maintain the excellence."

And excellence is always what Serrano is striving for. "My entire team has only one goal in mind," he says. "We want to give each and every guest the ultimate gastronomic experience."

Has he achieved that goal? "Today Picasso is the most healthy, popular, and the best we have ever been," he says. "That fulfills me. My philosophy is that life is what you make of it. If you have a good attitude, you will have a good life."

Life for Julian Serrano is so good, he made the cover of *Newsweek* magazine six years ago when Bellagio first opened. And then he won the James Beard Award for Best Chef in the Southwest Region, the only chef to win two of the prestigious regional awards, for Masa's and Picasso.

Warm Lobster Salad

with panache of tropical fruit and citrus vinaigrette

Serves 4

Lobster

4 1-lb.	lobsters
4	straight wooden sticks
kitchen string	
boiling water	

Panache of tropical fruit

1 large	mango, finely diced
1 large	papaya, finely diced
1 large	kiwi, finely diced
1 small	pineapple, finely diced

Salad

2 bunches	mâche lettuce
1 bunch	red oak lettuce
1 bunch	Belgian endive
1 head	curly endive
1 head	treviso (radicchio) lettuce
1 bunch	celery root, peeled and julienned
1 bunches	chervil leaves
2 tsp.	pink peppercorns
lobster oil	

Citrus vinaigrette

1/2 cup	blood-orange juice
1/2 cup	pineapple juice
1/2 cup	lemon juice
1/2 cup	lime juice
1 tbsp.	honey
1 tsp.	truffle juice
1 tsp.	port wine
1 tsp.	sherry vinegar
2 tsp.	extra virgin olive oil
salt and freshly ground pepper	

For the lobster:

• Tie the lobsters to a wooden stick to keep the tail straight while cooking.
• Poach the lobsters in the boiling water for two minutes. Remove from the water and cool.
• When cooled, remove the tail meat and slice into half-inch medallions (hold the tails while slicing to retain the tail shape). Remove the claw meat and set aside. Reserve the heads and tails for garnish.

For the vinaigrette:

• Individually reduce the fruit juices by half. The lime and lemon juices may be reduced together.
• Combine the reduced juices in a mixing bowl. Whisk in the honey, truffle juice, port, and sherry vinegar. Slowly whisk in the olive oil and season with salt and pepper to taste.

To complete:

• On four chilled plates, place the mâche lettuce leaves in a semi-circle at the top (12 o'clock position). Place the red oak lettuce leaves on top of the mâche. Top the red oak lettuce leaves with the curly endive.
• Toss the julienned celery root with some of the vinaigrette. Place the celery root at the center of the plates. Fan the Belgian endive leaves on the bottom of the plates (6 o'clock position). Place a leaf of treviso in the center of the endive fan.
• Warm the lobster meat in a sauté pan with some of the dressing. Arrange the medallions in a line over the celery root.
• Place the claws at 2 o'clock and 10 o'clock. Spoon warm salad dressing over the entire salad and garnish with chervil leaves, pink peppercorns, and lobster oil. Place one tablespoon of diced fruit on top of the lobster on each salad.

Wine pairing:

• Northern Rhone, Sauvignon Blanc

Roasted Filet of Halibut

with white and green asparagus and morel ragout

Serves 4

Morel ragout

40	fresh morel mushrooms
12 oz.	butter
2 tbsp.	shallots, chopped
1 cup	white wine
4 cups	chicken stock
4	Roma tomatoes, peeled, seeded, and diced
4 tsp.	parsley, chopped
salt and freshly ground pepper	

Asparagus jus

2 tbsp.	shallots, chopped
4 oz.	butter
4 cups	chicken stock
48 pcs.	green asparagus
salt and freshly ground pepper	
1/8 tsp.	nutmeg
2 tsp.	lemon juice

Halibut

4 5-oz.	halibut filets
1 cup	extra virgin olive oil
salt and freshly ground pepper	

The entrée

12 pcs.	white asparagus, peeled and blanched
12 pcs.	green asparagus, peeled and blanched
4 bunches	micro greens
1 tsp.	sherry vinegar
1 tbsp.	extra virgin olive oil
salt and freshly ground pepper	

For the morel ragout:
• Rinse the morels in cold water three times until all the grit is removed from the mushrooms. Place the mushrooms on a clean dry towel to drain.
• In a sauté pan over medium heat, sweat the shallots in the butter. Add the morels and cook for one minute. Add the white wine, increase the heat, and reduce by half. Add the chicken stock and cook until the mushrooms are tender.
• Add the tomato and parsley. Season to taste and set aside in a warm place.

For the asparagus jus:
• In a sauté pan over medium heat, place the shallots and butter. Slowly cook the shallots until translucent. Add the chicken stock and asparagus. Cook until tender and season with the salt and pepper to taste.
• Purée the mixture in a blender until smooth.
• Add the nutmeg and lemon juice. Set aside in a warm place.

For the halibut:
• In a sauté pan over medium-high heat, place the extra virgin olive oil. Season the halibut filets.
• Place the halibut in the hot oil skin side up and cook until lightly brown. Turn the fish filets over and place in a preheated 400° oven for a few minutes until the fish is cooked to your desired temperature.

To complete:
• Divide the asparagus jus onto the center of four warm plates. Arrange three white asparagus spears and three green asparagus spears over the jus on each plate.
• Place the halibut on top of the asparagus. Arrange the morels around.
• Toss the micro greens with the sherry vinegar, olive oil, salt, and pepper. Top the fish with the micro greens and serve.

Wine pairing:
• Sauvignon Blanc or Gruner Velt Liner

Honorio Mecinas

*2004 Award of Excellence,
Wine Spectator*

Think French brasserie—all gleaming Belle Epoque brass, rich maple paneling, and deep burgundy leather banquettes. Then think simple French bistro food—cassoulet and bouillabaisse and wild game—along with the consciousness-has-been-raised California penchant for adding a lighter touch to traditional French bistro fare.

Then meet 30-something Chef Honorio Mecinas, a native of Oaxaca, Mexico, and the creative center of Pinot Brasserie at the Venetian. Perhaps the youngest executive chef on the Vegas Strip, this unpretentious immigrant has caught the attention of foodies and critics and has garnered himself a national reputation.

Mecinas was 17 when he followed his three brothers from Mexico to the United States, unable to speak the language and possessing few marketable skills. He joined his brothers at Joachim Splichal's Pinot Bistro in Studio City, California, working as a potato peeler and carrot cutter. Mecinas found he loved the action in the kitchen. At one point the four Mecinas brothers stood shoulder-to-shoulder on the line, motivating each other to do better and applauding each other's successes.

Honorio had a natural talent in the kitchen and an eagerness to absorb everything he could. "I learned on the job," he says. "One station at a time. It might have been slower this way than going to school, but I didn't have the money."

His diligence paid off. Master Chef Joachim Splichal, who himself came to the United States in 1981 from Germany and now owns ten restaurants in California, recognized his talent and asked Mecinas to help him open Pinot Hollywood. After that, Mecinas was on a fast track to success with Café Pinot in California and, finally, Pinot Brasserie.

Mecinas takes none of it for granted and praises his mentor for giving him a chance to shine. "Joachim is a great teacher, fabulous chef, and brilliant businessman," he says. "I love being around him, because I continue to learn things every time we get together or speak on the phone."

Personal passion drives Mecinas to show his benefactor how happy he is by doing a great job on each and every plate. He loves nothing more than to jump into the cooking frenzy of the line when things get hectic. "I want to give others the opportunity Joachim gave to me," he says with his shy smile. "I want to be a better chef."

If Pinot Brasserie's chef isn't French, everything else about it's *très authentique*. Waiters wear traditional black vests and white aprons (and don rubber boots in the Oyster Bar). Splichal scoured the flea markets of Paris and Provence to find such treasures as antique mercury wall mirrors, the floor from a French chateau, and a 150-year-old wooden ceiling. Even the country scenes on the wall in one of the side dining rooms are from a butcher shop in Paris.

But the wooden entrance doors salvaged from a 19th century hotel in Monte Carlo are Splichal's pride and joy. "I wanted to bring something real to Vegas," he said. "Something that's already had a life in Europe for a hundred years and that will live on here."

He needn't have worried. When he brought Honorio Mecinas to Las Vegas, he brought a real chef. Mecinas may not last a hundred years, but his food at Pinot Brasserie is about as real as it gets.

Grilled Filet Mignon

with pommes gateau: potato cake, sautéed spinach, and foie gras red-wine sauce

Serves 4

3 large	Idaho potatoes
1/2 large	yellow onion
2 slices	bacon
1 tbsp.	crème fraiche or sour cream
1 pinch	salt
1 pinch	pepper
1 cup	all-purpose flour
2 whole	eggs
1 cup	bread crumbs
1/2 cup	vegetable oil
1 lb.	spinach
1 cup	beef stock
1 cup	red wine
foie gras	
4 8-oz.	filet mignon

For the pommes gateau:
• Peel and cut the potatoes in three pieces, then boil in water and salt until soft. Drain the water and mash the potatoes.
• Take 1/2 of yellow onion and finely dice. Cut 2 slices of bacon into small cubes. Cook the bacon in a sauté pan until crispy. Remove the bacon and cook the onions in the same pan using the bacon fat until caramelized. Return bacon to onions.
• Combine this with the potatoes and 1 tablespoon of crème fraiche or sour cream. Season with salt and pepper to taste.
• Form this into cake shape and dust with flour.
• Beat eggs in a bowl. Place breadcrumbs on a plate beside the egg bowl. Dip potato cakes in egg, then bread crumbs, and pan fry in vegetable oil until golden brown.

For the foie gras red-wine sauce
• Reduce beef stock and red wine.
• Quickly sauté the foie gras, strain out the fat, and add into the reduction sauce.

To complete:
• Sauté spinach with butter and garlic. Add salt and pepper to taste.
• Pre-heat your grill if necessary. Rub the filets with oil and salt and pepper.
• Grill until medium rare.
• Place the potato cake on the bottom of the plate. Layer with the spinach and place the filet on top. Serve the foie gras red-wine sauce over the top of the filet and pour a small amount around the plate.

Wine pairing:
• 2000 Honig Cabernet Sauvignon or Ferrari Carano Sienna Cabernet Sauvignon/ Sangiovese

Seared Foie Gras

with petit apricot French toast, vanilla orange butter, and micro greens

Serves 4

6 oz.	dried apricot pieces
1 cup	white wine
2 cups	apricot liquor
1 ea.	vanilla bean
2 cups	orange juice
2 oz.	unsalted butter
2 slices	brioche
4 3-oz.	pieces of foie gras
2 oz.	micro greens
black pepper and salt	

For the petit apricot French toast:
• Cut the apricot into small pieces. In a sauce pot, combine the apricot with white wine to cover and reduce to 1/2 or until the alcohol evaporates.
• Deglaze with apricot liquor, split the vanilla bean and add into reduction, then cover with orange juice, and cook until soft.
• Remove the apricots, keeping the liquid in the pot.
• Reduce down to half and add whipped butter until the juice gets syrupy.
• Spread the apricot mixture between two slices of brioche and toast in a skillet with butter until golden brown.
• Remove from pan and cut in four pieces. Set aside.

For the foie gras and to finish the entrée:
• Season the foie gras with black pepper and salt.
• In a hot skillet, sear the foie gras on both sides until golden brown and medium to medium-rare inside.
• Place foie gras next to the golden-brown apricot French toast.
• Add micro greens and drizzle the vanilla orange butter on the toast and the plate.

Wine pairing:
• 2000 Far Niente Dolce

Chef Honorio Mecinas © 2005 Pinot Brasserie

John LaGrone

2004 Award of Excellence, Wine Spectator

A mentor can be the spark that ignites the flame of creativity. That's how it was for John LaGrone. Growing up, he imagined himself becoming a cartoonist, but a little part of him was always drawn to cooking and he enjoyed experimenting with different recipes. At 19, he decided to try cooking school. "I studied at the California Culinary Academy," he says, "but the key was working with Wolfgang Puck at Postrio in San Francisco."

LaGrone began working under Puck as a prep cook while still in school and moved to full time on the line after graduation. "It was like boot camp, with on-the-job training 16 hours a day," he adds. "I loved it. I absorbed the experience like a sponge. Wolfgang infuses you with so many ideas—I'm always thinking out of the box."

As his talent became evident, LaGrone rose like a comet through the ranks of the Puck organization. He was entrusted with opening several Spago restaurants, including the one at Caesars Palace in Las Vegas before taking on Postrio at the Venetian. There, he's one of the youngest executive chefs, just over thirty, in the Puck empire. He credits his success to Puck's "leadership skills and the investment the organization makes in bringing you along and promoting from within."

But mentoring can only go so far; then it's up to the mentored. LaGrone has earned his toque with constant creativity and a fresh approach to food. "I like to keep pushing the envelope with new twists to traditional recipes and basic cuts of beef and chicken or fish," he says. "I get creative with the techniques and ingredients until I have something really wonderful. It's not hard to have a great dish when you're using the most expensive products. They key is being able to turn something plain and simple into a fantastic dish that surprises the palate."

Healthy creative cuisine is the way LaGrone describes his menu. "There's a big emphasis on low carbohydrates these days, so I incorporate more veggies and fewer sauces in the dishes," he says. "There are more baked or grilled offerings." But what really gets his juices flowing is braising. "Braised short ribs is my favorite dish," he says. "My friends kid me about my braised meats. I braise everything."

This tall genuine young man is a delightful blend of polished enthusiasm and high adrenaline. He has earned the respect of his staff, many older than he by a decade. On the floor of the restaurant, his eyes dart around the dining room as it fills up. He trades barbs with the restaurant manager, then dashes through the swinging doors to the kitchen, where he jumps into the line while calling out instructions to the sous chef and his crew. His loyal staff enjoys camaraderie even when the pressure is on to put out more than 350 dinners a night that would test the nerves of the most seasoned chef.

Postrio has become home to the power lunch, where deals are cut over the pumpkin ravioli with hazelnut brown butter, crisp sage, and parmesan or the prosciutto pizza with nicoise olives, chili flakes, and Sonoma goat cheese.

Casual diners enjoy sitting "outside" at the edge of the Venetian's St. Mark's Square (minus the pigeons), watching the carnivale of minstrel opera singers, "living"-artist sculpture, and various other street performers. Inside it's more formal. Warm polished-wood paneling and a lush burgundy carpet are accented with walls of hand-blown stained glass in hues of red, purple, and gold.

Postrio Salmon en Papillote

Serves 4

Salmon

1/2 cup	olive oil
2 bulbs	fennel, sliced thin
salt and black pepper	
4 7-oz.	salmon filets, skin and pin bones removed
4 sheets	thick parchment paper (or aluminum foil) cut each piece to be approx. 18" x 24"
8 tbsp.	shallot-herb butter, softened
12 ea.	Roma tomatoes, made into "petals" (skinned, seeded, quartered), marinated lightly in olive oil, black pepper, and salt
1/2 cup	shallots, sliced thin
8 medium	Fingerling or Yukon Gold potatoes, blanched in water until tender, peeled, and sliced
2 medium	parsnips, peeled, sliced thin on a bias
8 tbsp.	tomato sauce, fresh, infused with basil and garlic
8 sprigs	chervil (omit if unavailable)
8 sprigs	dill, fresh
8 sprigs	fresh Italian parsley
2 tbsp.	butter, melted

Shallot-herb butter

1 cup	unsalted butter, softened
1 tsp.	chervil, chopped
1 tsp.	dill, chopped
2 tsp.	Italian parsley, chopped
1 tbsp.	shallots, chopped fine
1/2 tsp.	lemon juice
1 tsp.	salt
1/4 tsp.	black pepper, fine

For the salmon:

• Heat a medium sauté pan to hot and add 1 tablespoon of olive oil. Carefully add half the fennel in a single layer. Season with salt and pepper and cook on both sides, turning once, over high heat until tender and well caramelized. Remove to a sheet pan and spread thin to cool.

• Repeat process with second half of the fennel. Cool completely.

• Repeat this process with the sliced parsnips. Set aside to cool.

• Season salmon filets with salt and pepper and set aside.

• Spread out each piece of parchment onto open counter space. Each piece will be folded in half lengthwise and the fish will sit right near the crease.

• Approximately 1" from the where the crease will go, spread 1 tablespoon of shallot-herb butter on either side (in a circle in the center of each half of the paper), so that when folded the butter will be both on top and on the bottom of the fish.

• On the bottom portion of the butter circle where the fish will be placed, arrange the vegetables (loosely), dividing them evenly into the four portions (shallots, fennel, parsnips, tomato petals, and potatoes). Include the tomato petals when placing the vegetables into the paper bag. Top them with tomato sauce.

• Top with the salmon filet. Place a little tomato sauce atop the salmon filet and arrange some of the chervil, dill, and parsley on the very top.

• On the outer 1" edge of the parchment, brush with the melted butter. Fold the top half of the paper over the salmon until the edges meet and roll the excess paper up toward the filet to seal well (roll only about 1 inch of the paper up). Crimp.

• Chill the salmon for at least 20 minutes or up to 4 hours.

• Preheat oven to 500°.

• Remove papillotes (salmon bags) from refrigerator 30 minutes before cooking.

• Place salmon en papillotes onto two cookie sheets and bake in oven for 14 minutes. For medium-rare salmon, bake for only 12 minutes. For well-done, bake for 18 minutes. Do not be alarmed if the parchment paper browns well.

For the shallot-herb butter:

• Combine all ingredients in a mixing bowl and mix well.

• Allow to stand at room temperature if using immediately or refrigerate for up to 24 hours before use.

• Place butter on paper in two circles.

• Top with vegetables and the fish portion on one half. Top the fish with the sauce and herbs, then brush the outside portion of the paper with melted butter.

- Fold the paper over and crimp the edges to form a seal.
- shallot butter,
- fish and melted
- folded paper
- crimp
- butter placement

Wine pairing:
- Red: Etude 2001 Pinot Noir, Williams Selyem 2001 Russian River Vineyard Pinot Noir or Classic Burgundy from France
- White: New Zealand Sauvignon Blanc or Albarino from Portugal

Step One

Step Two

Step Three

Braised Beef Short Ribs

with creamy rosemary polenta, Swiss chard, and pearl onions

Serves 4

Short ribs

4 16-oz.	beef short ribs, bone-in
1 pinch	salt
1 pinch	black pepper
1 cup	all-purpose flour
1/2 cup	olive oil
2 cloves	garlic, peeled and smashed lightly
1/2 cup	tomato paste
1 cup	white wine
1-1/2 cups	Madeira wine
4 cups	chicken stock
3/4 cup	veal demiglace

Mirepoix vegetables

1 cup	yellow onion, medium dice
1/2 cup	carrot, peeled, medium dice
1/2 cup	celery, medium dice

Sachet

25-30	whole black peppercorns
5 sprigs	fresh thyme
2 sprigs	fresh rosemary
3 sprigs	fresh Italian parsley, tied into a cheesecloth bag

Polenta

3 cups	water
1 cup	whole milk
1-1/2 tsp.	black pepper, fresh cracked
2 sprigs	rosemary, wrapped and tied into a cheesecloth
1 cup	coarse polenta
1/2 cup	mascarpone cheese
1/2 cup	parmesan cheese, high quality, grated fine
1 tbsp.	unsalted butter
2 tbsp.	olive oil
1 tbsp. + 1 tsp.	salt

Garnish

1 cup	white pearl onions
2 cups	green or red Swiss chard, washed, ribs removed, wide julienne
1 clove	garlic, minced
	olive oil

For the short ribs:

- Pre-heat oven to 350°.
- Season the short ribs with salt and pepper and dredge lightly in the flour. Pat off excess flour.
- Heat a sauté pan and add 2 tablespoons of olive oil. When oil is very hot, sear short ribs on both meat sides until well browned. Remove to a plate and set aside.
- Separately, heat a small stock pot and 2 tablespoons of oil. When the oil is very hot, add mirepoix vegetables and garlic and sauté. Reduce heat to medium and cook, stirring frequently, until vegetables caramelize. Add the tomato paste and cook on high for two more minutes, stirring almost constantly. Deglaze with the wines and reduce by one-third. Add both stocks and bring back to a boil. Add the sachet and return short ribs to the pot. Reduce heat to a simmer and season the braising liquid (it should be well-seasoned).
- Cover the pot tightly with aluminum foil and a lid, then place into pre-heated 350° oven for 2 to 2-1/2 hours, being sure to check the ribs after two hours. The ribs should be very tender and almost falling away from the bone when done. Remove ribs to a small roasting pan and strain the cooking liquid. Cover the ribs with the strained cooking liquid and keep warm in low oven until ready to serve.

For the polenta:

- Combine the water and milk in a large saucepot and bring to a rapid boil. Add the rosemary and salt. In a thin stream, steadily add the polenta, using a whisk to stir constantly.
- Once the polenta has been slowly incorporated, switch to a wooden spoon and stir constantly, lowering the heat to low. Cook the polenta for 25 minutes, adding more water if the mixture becomes very thick (the consistency should be thick, but no thicker than mashed potatoes).
- Remove from the heat, then stir in the butter, cheese, olive oil, and mascarpone. Remove the rosemary. Season with pepper and check the seasoning one final time. Serve immediately or keep warm in a warm water bath.

For the garnish:

- Combine the pearl onions (unpeeled) and 4 cups water in a medium saucepan. Season lightly with salt, place over high heat, and bring to a boil. Once the pot boils, turn off immediately and cover. Allow to sit for 10 minutes and strain, discarding the water.
- Spread the onions out on a towel to cool, then peel, using a knife to trim away the ends.

• Heat a medium sauté pan and add 1 tablespoon of olive oil. Add the onions and allow to cook over medium heat for 3-4 minutes until they caramelize on one side. Season with salt.

• Separately heat another sauté pan on high and add 1 tablespoon of olive oil. Add the garlic first, then immediately the chard and sauté until tender, about a minute. Make sure that the chard spreads to touch the surface of the pan and doesn't "clump" together.

To complete:

• Spoon 1 cup of cooked polenta onto the center of each warm serving plate. Top with the warm short ribs and spoon some of the cooking liquid over.

• Place some chard and caramelized pearl onions onto each plate to garnish and serve immediately.

Wine pairing:

• Chateau Julian 2000 Red Zinfandel, Gloria Ferrar 2000 Syrah of California, or Fonthill 2002 Dust of Ages Grenache

Chef John LaGrone © 2005 Postrio

Wendy Jordan
Michael Jordan

Sante's 2003 Wine & Spirits
Cooking Restaurant of the Year

It might have been love at first bite. Michael and Wendy Jordan met as students at the Culinary Institute of America and you just know these foodies must have tasted each other's cooking by at least the second date.

One bite usually leads to another when two culinary talents get together, and soon this duo had won their toques from the Institute, even as they were winning each other's hearts. They wed, toured Europe, and settled down in New Orleans to perfect their cooking skills. Michael joined the team of Emeril Lagasse. "In his kitchen, my education from CIA was molded into technique," he says. "I was introduced to countless ingredients and different types of product. I learned how to marry wine with food and how to give great front-of-the-house service. Most important, I learned about loyalty and a sense of being a part of something great."

Meanwhile, Chef Wendy studied with Susan Spicer of bayona and John Neal of Peristyle. "They both have classic French style," she says. "The foods from the south of France are so exciting to me. It's a very fresh element of French cuisine. I really connected with that."

Lagasse sent Michael as executive chef to open the first Emeril restaurant in Las Vegas at the MGM Grand Hotel and Casino. Wendy started her own successful catering company. But these two always knew they wanted to be in the kitchen together, and in 1999 they opened their own restaurant, named for Michael's mother, off the Vegas Strip. It soon became a hangout for locals. By 2002 they were so successful they opened Rosemary's at the Rio, at the Rio All-Suites Hotel and Casino just west of the Strip (since closed). The awards have piled up and the Jordans have become regular television guest celebrity chefs.

Michael credits his Grandmother Jordan for developing his appreciation for the kitchen. "I would wake up with her at 5 a.m. as she began her day cooking for the family," he remembers. "It was the only time we had alone together and that time in the kitchen was really special to me. I grew up understanding that being in a kitchen or preparing food for someone was one of the best ways to 'speak' with them."

The Jordans' food is creative and calls forth their personal history. "The Creole cuisine of New Orleans has influenced me the most," says Michael. Wendy's childhood is fondly remembered in Hugo's barbecue shrimp at Rosemary's. "My dad created the recipe for the barbecue sauce, so I grew up loving that flavor," says Wendy. "It's the perfect blend of texture and flavor: crispy seared shrimp, bleu cheese, and barbecue sauce." Local farmers supply products to Rosemary's.

When it comes to ingredients, the Jordans have strong opinions. "Foie gras is the finest ingredient in the world!" intones Michael. "Butter," counters Wendy. "There's no substitute for enhancing flavor." Michael also likes to use duck. "It can add such a depth to a dish," he says. And he likes mushrooms—"morels and chanterelles, especially the chanterelles from Louisiana, because they're moist and have a hint of apricot to them." Wendy likes the flavor parmesan cheese can add to a dish. Her favorite spice is tarragon.

The ambience at Rosemary's is warm and cozy. Art on the wall showcases local artists. Sitting at the bar you can look into the kitchen and watch your dinner being prepared—and keep an eye on that couple hanging out together.

Grilled Wild King Salmon

on an apple-fennel slaw with a toasted walnut vinaigrette

Serves 4

Salmon

4 6-oz.	wild king salmon, marinated 2 hours to 3 days (recipe follows)
1/2 cup	peanut oil
1 pinch	salt
1 pinch	white pepper

Slaw

1 medium	Granny Smith apple, peeled and quartered
2 cup	green cabbage, shaved thin
1/4	fennel bulb, shaved thin
1/4 cup	walnut vinaigrette
2 tbsp.	green onions, shaved thin
1 pinch	salt
1 pinch	white pepper

Salmon marinade

1/2 cup + 2 tbsp.	loosely packed fresh basil leaves, blanched and chopped
1/4 cup	preserved lemon, chopped
1 quart	peanut oil
1 tsp.	white pepper, ground

Walnut vinaigrette

3/4 cup	walnuts
1 small	shallot, finely diced
2 tbsp.	honey
1/2 cup	cider vinegar
2 cup	peanut oil
1 cup	walnut oil
2 tbsp.	chives, minced
salt and white pepper to taste	

Candied walnuts

4	egg whites
1 tbsp.	water
1-1/2 cups	sugar
1 sheet	parchment paper
1 tsp.	salt
1 tsp.	cinnamon
2 cup	walnut nuggets

For the salmon:
- Using two large sauté pans, add just enough peanut oil to cover the bottom of each pan and place over medium heat.
- Season the salmon to taste with salt and white pepper. When the oil smokes, add the salmon to the pans. Leave them alone until a good crust forms, then turn them over. Cook to medium-rare (or your preferred degree of doneness).
- Remove to a plate, cover, and keep warm until needed.

For the slaw:
- Grate the Granny Smith apple. In a medium bowl, combine the grated apple with the cabbage, fennel, walnut vinaigrette, and green onions.
- Toss well and season with salt and white pepper. Adjust seasoning to taste.

For the marinade:
- Using a blender, combine the basil, lemon, 1 cup of the peanut oil, and the white pepper and purée very well. Add the purée to the remaining oil and stir well. Makes 1 quart.

For the walnut vinaigrette:
- Toast the walnuts at 325° until golden brown.
- Meanwhile, combine the shallot, honey, and vinegar in a blender. Turn blender on and slowly add the oils.
- Pour the vinaigrette over the warm walnuts and stir in the chives. Taste and season with salt and white pepper. Makes 1 quart.

For the candied walnuts:
- Preheat oven to 225°. Beat the egg whites with the water just to loosen the whites. Add the sugar and seasonings and stir well to combine. Roll the nuts in the mixture and spread onto an oiled sheet of parchment paper placed on a cookie sheet. Bake for 1 hour, stirring every 15 minutes.
- Once they're done, remove from the oven and stir again as they cool to coat the nuts completely with the mixture.
- Cool before storing. Makes 2 cups.

For the port-wine syrup:
- Place 1/2 of the bottle of port wine in a saucepot and reduce slowly until wine is thick, like a syrup.
- To check, place a small plate in the freezer for 5 minutes and drizzle a bit of the syrup onto the plate.
- If it doesn't run, it's done. Makes about 1/4 cup.

DIFFICULTY LEVEL: 5

Port-wine syrup

1 bottle	port wine

To complete:

1 cup	walnut vinaigrette
1/2 cup	honey (the best quality possible)
1/2 cup	candied walnuts
4 tbsp.	port-wine syrup

To complete:

- Using four warm entrée plates, ladle 1/4 cup of walnut vinaigrette onto each plate.
- Place the slaw in the middle of the plate.
- Top the slaw with the salmon.
- Drizzle each portion of salmon with a little of the honey and sprinkle with the candied walnuts and a little of the port-wine syrup.

Wine pairing:

- Yellow Tail 2002 The Reserve Chardonnay

Grilled Double-Cut Pork Chops

with Hoppin' John and Creole-mustard reduction

Serves 4

Pork Chops

6 12-oz.	pork chops
1/2 cup	canola oil
1 tbsp.	black pepper, ground
1 tbsp.	kosher salt
16 oz.	veal jus
3 tbsp.	Creole mustard
2 tbsp.	dark brown sugar
1 tsp.	white pepper, ground
1 tbsp.	butter
1 cup	apple-smoked bacon, sliced and cooked, drain well
1 cup	green onion, green only, shaved thin
1 recipe	sweet brine
1 recipe	Hoppin' John

Sweet brine for pork

7 cups	water
1/2 cup	kosher salt
1/2 cup	dark brown sugar
1 tbsp.	molasses
2 cups	ice

Hoppin' John

1/4 cup	bacon fat
1-1/2 cups	yellow onion, small diced
1 cup	green bell pepper, small diced
1 cup	celery, small diced
1 cup	green onion, shaved thin
2 cups	long grain rice
1 whole	bay leaf
4 cups	white chicken stock
10 sprigs	fresh thyme
2 tsp.	white pepper
2 oz.	butter
1 cup	black-eyed peas, cooked
1 cup	apple-smoked bacon, sliced and cooked crispy (reserve the fat to cook the rice)

For the Creole-mustard reduction:

• Combine the veal jus with the mustard and brown sugar. Bring to a boil, skim well, and simmer for 15 minutes. Taste. Adjust seasoning with salt, white pepper, a little more sugar or mustard, and finish with the butter.

• Strain through a fine mesh strainer and hold in a water bath until pork chops are ready.

For the sweet brine:

• Combine all ingredients but the meat. Stir well to dissolve the sugars. Add the pork chops and brine for 4 hours.

For the Hoppin' John:

• In a large saucepan, melt the bacon fat. Add the onions, bell pepper, and celery. Cover with a lid and turn the heat to low to sweat the vegetables.

• When the vegetables are soft, add the green onion, rice, bay leaf, chicken stock, and thyme. Bring to a boil, and add some salt and pepper.

• Cover with a lid, turn the heat to low, and cook for 15 minutes. Remove from the heat and allow to rest for 5 minutes. Fold in the butter, black-eyed peas, and bacon. Taste and adjust the seasoning, if needed.

• Hold in warm spot until you're ready to finish the entrée.

To complete:

• Heat the grill.

• Remove the chops from the brine, rinse, and dry well.

• Toss the chops with canola oil, salt, and black pepper.

• Place all the chops onto the hot grill with the bone facing 2 o'clock. After 5 minutes, turn the bone facing 10 o'clock.

• After 5 more minutes, flip the pork chop over with the bone at 2 o'clock. After about 5 minutes, turn the bone to 10 o'clock.

• Remove the pork chops and allow to rest for another 5 minutes.

• Spoon some Hoppin' John into the middle of the plate.

• Place a pork chop against the rice. Ladle a little more sauce over the pork chop and garnish with the bacon, green onions, and some ground black pepper on the rim of the plate.

Wine pairing:

• Boroli (Bricco 4 Fratelli) Barbera 'd Alba 1999

Kerry Simon

It all started because Kerry Simon, in his late teens, wanted to play rock and roll. To finance an electric guitar, he got a job slinging pizza dough at Little Caesar's in Chicago. It may be poetic justice that Simon now appears nightly at the Hard Rock Hotel & Casino—but he's exchanged his guitar for pots and pans as he turns out an innovative cuisine that has made him an international celebrity.

"My path to cooking came about in a winding, almost fateful, way," Simon explains. His taste for restaurants whetted, he applied to the Culinary Institute of America, but his name wasn't called for five years. "I thought I was not meant to be a chef," he says. "Then they called. I had to be ready for classes in a month." He scraped the money together and found his passion. "I couldn't get the information fast enough," he adds. "As I learned more, I wanted more. This became my life."

His life has included some of the best restaurants in the world—La Cote Basque, Lutece, and The Plaza Hotel in New York City, along with Miami's Blue Star, Starfish, and Max's South Beach. He served a stint in both London and New York as a personal chef to the wealthy. In 1998 he opened Prime, the steakhouse at Bellagio. I've worked with some of the best chefs in the world," he says. "Each one left an impression on me and I credit all of them with helping me become a better chef."

Simon's cooking has gathered an armload of awards, including a triple crown of Epicurean Awards for Best New Restaurant, Best Desserts, and New Chef of 2003. He's been credited with creating food trends that include fusion,

comfort food, and now New American cuisine, which has a touch of Thai, a hint of Italian, a soupçon of French, and even a pinch of Indian curry. But the awards don't faze him. "That's not what I'm about," he explains. With Zen-like calm Simon talks of becoming a chef as "a process to find a career that is as painful in its exploration of truth and failures as it is rewarding in personal satisfaction."

All this experience has brought him to his own trendy, quirky restaurant—a hang-out kind of place, swank and sleek, where the waiters wear designer blue jeans and the menu features everything from meat loaf to pumpkin soup with applewood-smoked bacon and sage (and even that all-American favorite, macaroni and cheese). "By using a handful of simple sauces and broths, we enable the diner to experience food's natural intense flavors," Simon says. "As a result, the dishes themselves end up lighter, fresher."

He loves to use ingredients like limes, all types of citrus, and cilantro with seafood and vegetables. Lightness is his mantra, and he's replaced traditional heavy sauces with low-fat ingredients and an innovative mix of bold flavors.

Kerry Simon's originality comes from a deep sense of himself. "Keep imagining," he says. "The attention is irrelevant; it's about fulfillment for yourself."

In the restaurant, Simon keeps no secrets from his customers: The kitchen is in full view and diners can watch all the action. Or they can sit by the wall of windows or on the sunny patio that overlook the jungle foliage surrounding the Hard Rock's lavish pool.

Chicken Curry

Serves 4

Chicken curry

4 large	chicken breasts, boneless, skinless, diced
1 large	carrot, peeled and diced
1 large	russet potato, peeled and diced
1 cup	fresh English peas
1/2 bunch	cilantro, rough chopped

Curry base

1/4 cup	vegetable oil
1 large	onion, rough chopped
3 large	celery stalks, rough chopped
1 large	carrot, peeled and chopped
1 inch	ginger root, chopped
1 leaf	Kaffir or regular lime leaf
2 tbsp.	curry powder
1 tbsp.	curry paste
2 quarts	chicken stock
1 15-oz.	can of unsweetened coconut milk
1 large	banana, slightly browned, chopped
salt and pepper	

Almond jasmine rice

2 cups	jasmine rice
2-1/2 cups	water
2 tbsp.	toasted-almond slivers

Tandoori chicken skewers

1 large	chicken breast, boneless, skinless
1 tsp.	plain yogurt
2 tbsp.	tandoori seasoning
4	bamboo skewers

Pineapple chutney

1/2 small	pineapple, peeled and diced small
1 medium	pear, peeled and diced
1 medium	red-bell pepper, diced small
1 cup	dried currants
2 tbsp.	brown sugar
1/4 cup	rice wine vinegar

For the almond jasmine rice:

- Rinse the rice under running water until the water runs clear, about three times.
- Combine the washed rice and the 2-1/2 cups water in a saucepan. Bring to a boil, cover, reduce the heat, and simmer until the water is absorbed. The rice should be tender and fluffy.
- Add almonds to the rice and stir in. Reserve, covered, in a warm place until you complete the entrée.

For the curry base:

- Heat the oil in a large sauté pan. Cook the onion, celery, and carrots over moderate heat until tender. Lightly season with salt and pepper.
- Add the ginger root and lime leaf. Cook until the ginger becomes fragrant. Add curry powder and cook, stirring, about 1 minute. Add curry paste and cook, stirring an additional minute.
- Add the chicken stock and increase heat to high. Bring to a boil and simmer until reduced by half.
- Add the coconut milk, bring to a boil, and simmer for 15 minutes. Add the banana and remove from heat.
- Purée the curry base, strain through a fine chinoise, and set aside.

For the pineapple chutney:

- Place all the ingredients in a small sauce pan. Cook the mixture until it's almost dry, stirring frequently.
- Cool mixture until ready to serve. This may be made several days ahead and stored in the refrigerator.

For the cucumber raita:

- In a small bowl, stir together the ingredients.
- Taste the raita and season with salt and fresh-ground pepper.

For the tandoori chicken skewers:

- Cut the chicken breast into strips. In a small bowl, combine the tandoori seasoning and the yogurt. Add the chicken and coat with the seasoning paste.
- Thread the chicken strips onto the bamboo skewers and refrigerate until ready to grill and garnish the entrée.

For the chicken curry:

- In a pot of boiling salted water, blanch the potatoes until 3/4 of the way cooked. Place the potatoes in ice water to stop the cooking, drain, and set aside. Repeat with the carrots and English peas.

Cucumber raita

1 medium	hothouse cucumber, peeled, seeded, and finely grated
1/2 cup	plain yogurt
1 tbsp.	cilantro, rough chopped
	salt and ground white pepper

- In a hot pan, sauté the chicken until browned, but not cooked through. Deglaze with a small amount of chicken stock and set aside.
- In a sauce pan, combine the chicken, potatoes, carrots, curry base, and cilantro. Bring to a simmer and finish cooking the chicken and vegetables. Add the peas. Taste and season with salt and pepper.

To complete:
- Grill the tandoori chicken skewers.
- Mound the jasmine rice onto four warmed plates.
- Arrange the chicken curry around the rice and garnish with the skewers.
- Accompany the entrée with small bowls of pineapple chutney, cucumber raita and pappadam bread.

Wine pairing:
- Pinot Grigio Santa Margherita 2000

Ahi Tuna with Soy Caramel Sauce

Serves 4

Ahi tuna

2 lbs.	Center-cut ahi loin, 1+ grade, cut into 8-oz. pieces
4 large	baby bok choy
salt and pepper	

Soy caramel sauce

2 cups	low-sodium soy sauce
1 cup	mirin
1 head	garlic, peeled
1/2 lb.	fresh ginger, peeled and chopped
3 large	shallots, peeled and sliced
3 tbsp.	pickled ginger, roughly chopped
1 tbsp.	unsalted butter

Wasabi mashed potatoes

1 lb.	Yukon Gold potatoes, peeled and cut in half
1/4 lb.	unsalted butter
1 cup	heavy cream
1 tbsp.	wasabi powder
3 tbsp.	water
salt	

Spicy shiitake mushrooms

1/2 cup	soy sauce
1/2 cup	mirin
1/2 tsp.	Sambal chili paste
1 tsp.	sesame oil
1/2 tbsp.	cilantro, chopped
8 large	shiitake mushrooms, stems removed

For the sauce:
• Combine all the ingredients except the pickled ginger.
• Bring to a boil and simmer until reduced by half. Strain through a fine chinois.
• Add the pickled ginger and butter. Set aside.

For the wasabi mashed potatoes:
• Boil the potatoes in a large pot of salted water.
• Cook until tender. When cooked, pour through a colander and drain the water. Put the potatoes through a food mill.
• While potatoes are cooking, mix the wasabi and water to form a paste. Reserve.
• In a small sauce pan, bring the cream and butter to a boil.
• Mix the potatoes, hot cream, and wasabi together until well incorporated. Reserve.

For the spicy shitake mushrooms:
• Combine all the ingredients together and marinate the mushrooms for about 1 hour.
• Sauté the mushrooms until tender and browned.
• Add water if necessary to prevent the mushrooms from burning. Reserve.

For the ahi tuna and to complete:
• In a pot of boiling salted water, blanch the bok choy and cut in half. Reserve.
• Season the ahi with salt and pepper.
• In a smoking hot pan, add oil and sear the ahi on all sides. Remove from the pan and slice.
• Place a scoop of wasabi mashed potatoes, two pieces of bok choy, two mushrooms, and the sliced ahi on a plate and drizzle with soy caramel sauce.

Wine pairing:
• Josmeyer Le Kottabe Alsace 2001

Chef Kerry Simon © 2005 Simon Kitchen and Bar

SPIEDINI RISTORANTE
JW Marriott and Rampart Casino

Gustav Mauler

A photograph of Gustav Mauler at five years old clearly predicts his future. The little Viennese boy is dressed in chef's whites, complete with toque. He recalls those early years, cooking side by side with his mother: "She was a wonderful cook who inspired me and gave me a great gift."

Mauler began his training at the Innkeeper School in Vienna and became a Certified Master Chef at the American Culinary Federation. He has worked at major restaurants from South Africa to Norway and from Atlantic City to Seattle. "I love to travel and watch and learn in the kitchens of other great chefs," he says. "I like to take the European ideas and bring them home with the American palate in mind."

In 1987, he came to Las Vegas. "When I came, the city was definitely not recognized for its culinary fare," he remembers. "We had to overcome many obstacles to get where we are today."

In Las Vegas, Mauler oversaw the development, planning, and design of all kitchens and restaurants within Mirage Resorts properties, including the Golden Nugget, Treasure Island, and the first phase of Bellagio. "I created a system and a process that allowed the kitchen to flow more easily," he says. "I studied other restaurant facilities and saw that we were putting out twice as many dinners in half the time. I went to each station—dishwasher, prep, garnishee—and asked how I could make their jobs easier. My system made everyone work better and the management of the cooking improved."

In 1999, Mauler launched his flagship restaurant, Spiedini at JW Marriott, under his own restaurant-development firm, Gustav International Chartered. Within two years, he added Sazio at the Orleans and BullShrimp at Green Valley Ranch. The word Spiedini is Italian for "skewer," and the restaurant's specialty is spit-roasted meats. "The turn of the spit bastes the meat in its own juices and makes it tender," he notes. His preference is for simple dishes, using marjoram, thyme, and chervil for subtle flavor. He offers a tip: "A little nutmeg in mashed potatoes is good."

Mauler's cooking has brought fame, television celebrity, and numerous awards. But chef duty is not the only pot on his stove. Working with Pulte Homes Nevada and General Electric, Mauler created an upgrade kitchen package called the Gustav Mauler Seal of Approval Kitchen, featuring GE Monogram equipment. "I'm focusing on designing kitchen spaces with minimal upgrades, but common sense ideas," he says. "For twenty years home designers gave little thought to the kitchen layout and flow. I think about where you come in, where you drop off your groceries, and if you have to circle like crazy to make a meal."

Despite his many successes, Mauler says he tries never to forget his roots. "I was born on November 1st, which is All Saints Day in Austria," he says. "That is the holiday when you pray for the dead. Every year, the relatives would come to celebrate my birthday, and they would be crying and hugging and kissing me. It was a crazy funny thing, but a blessing nonetheless."

The modern sophisticated décor of Spiedini gives it an elegantly casual atmosphere. The dining room is filled with art glass, mosaic tiles, and brightly colored hand-blown Venetian glass lighting fixtures that accent rich blonde woods. Vases overflow with fresh flowers. Guests may also dine alfresco on the tropical patio beside lush palm trees and waterfalls.

Spaghetti Alla Chitara

Serves 4

1 lb.	sweet Italian sausage, removed from casing
1 large	eggplant, peeled, cut into julienne
1/2 cup	white wine
2 cloves	garlic, chopped
2 tbsp.	fresh basil, chopped
2 cups	crushed tomatoes or marinara sauce
4 5-oz.	packages of fresh spaghetti
1/4 cup	shaved parmesan cheese
1 oz.	extra virgin olive oil
salt and pepper	

For the chitara sauce:

• Gently cook the morsels of sausage in a hot sauté pan for a few minutes until nicely browned. Remove the sausage from the pan and set aside. Drain the excess fat.

• Add the eggplant strips to the sausage pan, and brown. Add the garlic, then deglaze the pan with white wine.

• Add the basil and crushed tomatoes or marinara sauce and cook for 5 minutes. Set aside.

To complete:

• Cook homemade spaghetti in boiling, lightly salted water for no more than 3 minutes. (Cook ready-made spaghetti according to package instructions.)

• Drain, then toss with the sauce.

• Arrange the pasta on warm plates.

• Add lightly shaved parmesan to the top of the pasta. Drizzle with virgin olive oil.

Wine pairing:

• Merlot, Sangiovese, or Super Tuscan

Chef Gustav Mauler © 2005 Spiedini Restorante

Breast of Chicken Involtini

Serves 4

Chicken

4 6-oz.   chicken breast

Chicken breast filling

1 whole   red pepper, roasted, peeled,
             and cut into quarters.
4 oz.   spinach
4 oz.   fontina cheese
1 medium portobello mushroom
1/4 cup   olive oil
salt and pepper

Chicken breading

4 tbsp.   cake flour
2 whole   eggs
2 cups   Panko Asian crumbs

For the chicken filling:
- Quickly sauté the spinach just until wilted. Season with salt and pepper, then chill.
- Roast the red pepper, peel off the skin, and quarter.
- Use spoon to remove the beard from the portobello mushroom, then cut into quarters.
- Slice the fontina cheese.

For the chicken breasts:
- Pound each skinless, boneless chicken breast lightly.
- Place plastic wrap on worktable, lay out chicken breasts, and fill with spinach, roasted red pepper, fontina cheese, and portobello mushroom.
- Roll up into a log and set aside.
- Season chicken rolls with salt and pepper.

For the chicken breading:
- First, roll in flour gently, dip into beaten egg, then into the Panko crumbs. Chicken should be completly covered.
- Heat oil in a deep sauté pan.
- Sprinkle a few crumbs into the pan to see if the oil is hot enough.
- Cook chicken rolls on all sides for a few minutes and brown until golden.
- Place in a baking dish and finish cooking for 15 minutes in a 375° oven.

To complete:
- Slice into 1" thick rounds.
- Lay out on plate and serve with your favorite vegetable.

Wine pairing:
- Chalk Hill Chardonay: Chalk Hill Estate Vineyard 2001, or Renwood Zinfandel Amador County Old Vine 2001

DIFFICULTY LEVEL: 3

Chef Gustav Mauler © 2005 Spiedini Restorante

Mario Andreoni

"I hate all the stuff—the sauces and gravies—people put on food today," says Executive Chef Mario Andreoni. "Too much butter, too much garlic. It takes away from the taste." His goal is to give the customer "value in every bite—make it delicate and make it with care."

Andreoni credits Giovanni Spaventa (former executive chef of Cipriani Hotel in Venice, Italy), whom he calls the number-one chef in Italy, with this philosophy of simplicity. "He most influenced my style," says Andreoni. "No butter, no cream, just fresh. Cook it simply and season with salt and pepper. Use the best products and you can't go wrong. The difference between Northern Italy and Southern Italy is the spices. The heavy taste of Southern cooking makes it overpowering."

Italian-born Andreoni began his career as a chef in 1974, working in Venice. "Then I wanted to learn more than the Italian technique, so I moved to Paris and worked in a five-star restaurant," he says. There he found that French, Italian, and Mediterranean cooking all shared a respect for the finest quality ingredients prepared in a simple, yet elegant, manner that allowed the natural flavors to come through. After another stint in Venice, he felt it was time to expand his culinary thinking. "I went to the Dominican Republic, where I learned all different tastes and a mix of many ethnic specialties," he says.

Now he calls his cuisine "Simple Continental. It's the best from every cuisine done to the taste of the American palate," he explains. "I use thyme, marjoram, put in a little olive oil and enjoy. I let the food speak for itself. You do not have to fuss when the quality is there." It may be an anomaly in the middle of the desert, but fresh seafood is one of Andreoni's favorite ingredients, and it's readily available. "The freshest fish can be had here in Las Vegas," he says. "I call the vendor and the product arrives the next day."

Cooking for more than 300 people every night is a challenge for any chef. To maintain quality and consistency, Andreoni uses his own personal standards. "When I cook, I think, 'this is for me,'" he says. "It has to be good enough for me to eat, then I know I have done my best for the guest. I try to do it 100 percent every day."

But no chef stands alone at the stove. "I have a great team that I depend on all the time," notes Andreoni. "I love to help them grow. Like a workshop, the training is step by step." When he first became executive chef, he discovered the breadth of knowledge required by the one who runs the kitchen. "The food is only forty percent of the job. The executive chef must learn the budget, staff, people skills, P & L, ordering. The hardest part for me when I became executive chef was to learn that not everyone works like me. You have to watch everything and inspire people to do better at their job."

Top of the World rates with the best in Las Vegas when it comes to ambience. Your ears pop as you ascend the elevator to the 800-foot-high restaurant. Floor-to-ceiling windows look out on the highest panorama available in the valley. But there's more to come. Lest you tire of one scene, the restaurant revolves 360° every hour-and-a-half. The magnificent view provides stiff competition for the diner's attention, but Andreoni is up to it—the view plus his fabulous food come together to create one of Las Vegas' most impressive dining experiences.

Sea Bass with Fava Beans

Serves 4

Fava beans

1 cup	fava beans, soaked and peeled
2 tbsp.	olive oil
8 oz.	yellow tear-drop tomatoes
	fresh ground pepper

Coriander crust

2 oz.	coriander seed
2 oz.	bread crumbs
4 tbsp.	olive oil

Sea bass

| 4 8-oz. | sea bass filets |

Sauces

| 4 tbsp. | lemon truffle oil |
| 2 cups | balsamic vinegar |

For the coriander crust:
• Crack the coriander and mix with bread crumbs in large bowl. Slowly mix in the olive oil until the bread crumbs bind together.

For the sauce:
• In a small sauce pan, bring the balsamic vinegar to a slow simmer. Cook over low heat until it reaches the consistency of syrup. Set aside.

For the sea bass:
• Season the fish filets with salt and pepper. Top the filets with the breadcrumb mixture and bake for 7 minutes in a preheated 300° oven.

To complete:
• Heat the olive oil in a sauté pan. Add the fava beans and sauté for 1 minute. Add the tomatoes and toss to heat.
• Place beans and tomatoes at the center of four warm plates. Place the sea bass on top of the beans and drizzle the balsamic vinegar reduction around the plate.
• Drizzle the lemon truffle oil on and around the fish.

Wine pairing:
• Trimbach Pinot Gris Alsace

DIFFICULTY LEVEL: 2

Chef Mario Andreoni © 2005 Top of the World

Colorado Rack of Lamb

Serves 2

Rack of lamb

1 1-lb.	Colorado lamb rack, frenched
2 oz.	Creole mustard
4 oz.	Herbs de Provence crust
3 tbsp.	extra virgin olive oil
1 oz.	kosher salt
fresh ground pepper	

Curry sauce

3 oz.	carrots
3 oz.	onions
3 oz.	Granny Smith apples
3 oz.	bananas
1 cup	coconut milk
1/2 cup	tomato paste
1/2 cup	brandy
1 quart	chicken stock
1 oz.	Indian curry powder
1 cup	heavy whipping cream

For the lamb:
• Sear the lamb rack 3 minutes on each side, then let rest 5 minutes.
• Brush the lamb with Creole mustard, then coat the lamb with the crust mixture.
• Preheat oven to 350°. Roast the lamb for 18-20 minutes.
• Rest the lamb for 5 minutes.

For the curry sauce:
• Roast all the ingredients together (except the liquids).
• Add the brandy and flame out the alcohol.
• Add the chicken stock and cream, then simmer for 25-30 minutes.
• Purée the sauce until smooth.

For the Herbs de Provence crust:
• Combine thyme, rosemary, tarragon, mixed Herbs de Provence, fresh roasted garlic, and Japanese Panko bread crumbs in food processor until finely ground.

To complete:
• Place curry sauce on hot plate.
• Cut lamb into 2 double chops and place in center of plate.
• Add garnishes (roasted potatoes or artichokes, sautéed onions).

Wine pairing:
• Chateau Timberlay Bordeaux

Chef Mario Andreoni © 2005 Top of the World

Luciano Pellegrini

*2004 James Beard Foundation
Best Chef-Southwest Region
Grand Award Wine Spectator*

Ask for the "wild child" at Valentino and the smiling lively eyed Luciano Pellegrini will appear. He earned his nickname working in the kitchens of Piero Selvaggio, owner of Primi, the famous all-appetizer restaurant in Los Angeles, for whom he has been turning out innovative twists on traditional Italian cuisine for nearly 20 years.

Selvaggio credits Pellegrini with "pushing the envelope" in terms of Italian cooking. "Maybe he calls me wild child because I don't like to follow the rules," offers Pellegrini. "I have a rebellious streak." That rebellion has led him to experiment with flavors and textures that take Italian food to a whole new level and has turned the spotlight on its creator. After Primi, Pellegrini was chosen to open Selvaggio's prestigious Posto in Los Angeles. Finally, Selvaggio made him a partner in Valentino when the restaurant opened in the Venetian in Las Vegas in 1999.

Selvaggio isn't the only one to recognize Pellegrini's rebellious creative talent. For six years he was listed as one of the James Beard Award's Top 10 chefs in Los Angeles. When Valentino opened, the James Beard Foundation nominated Pellegrini for "Best Chef in the Southwest" honors in 2003 and awarded him the distinction in 2004.

The wild child's interest in cooking began at home in his native mountain village of Bergamo, Italy, when he was barely as high as his mother's apron strings. He went on to the celebrated San Pellegrino Hotel School when he was 13 and did his stint in the local restaurants during the summers. At age 18, he took a compulsory leave from the stove when he was drafted for military service and trained as a parachutist.

A year later, it was back to the real passion of his life—the kitchen. A friend enticed him to the United States and a job with Selvaggio. During his rise in the organization, he returned to Italy to study with the great chefs of his home country. He brought back new ideas for sausage making, wood grilling, and preparing seafood. "I love working with king crab and all types of fish," says Pellegrini. "You can really alter the taste by how you cook the fish, how you season it, or how you change the side dish."

Despite his reputation for reinterpreting traditional Italian foods, Pellegrini doesn't rely on exotic spices and herbs. "My spices are usually very light to almost nothing—a little salt and pepper," he says. "Great food should not need a lot of extra stuff. I don't like heavy sauces with so much spice that you can't taste the base." Some of his favorite dishes are fresh homemade pasta, polenta, and quail.

"I never want to lose sight of the passion," Pellegrini says. "This is not a job. There is no time clock, so you'd better love it for what it's all about—the food, the people, and pleasing one with the other.

"Through hard times and good ones, gratification in a job well done is the only reward most chefs get. It takes a long time to achieve a level of success, and that never really comes close to the hours we put in."

The sleekly deco, birch-paneled Valentino, with its Venetian glass vases and fabrics from Milan, is a stylish backdrop for Pellegrini's sophisticated cuisine. It encourages diners to go a little wild themselves. Why not sample something truly different like the frico—those bet-you-can't-eat-just-one parmesan chips fresh from the griddle. That's some kind of Italian!

Black Garganelli

with jumbo lump crab meat, bottarga, and leek purée

Serves 6

Sauce

14 oz.	jumbo lump crab
1 tbsp.	roasted garlic
2 tbsp.	butter
2 tbsp.	extra virgin olive oil
3 oz.	sliced bottarga
fresh thyme	

Leek purée

2	leeks
1/3 cup	extra virgin olive oil
1 tbsp.	roasted garlic
1/4 cup	white wine
1/2 cup	cream

Pasta

1 lb.	all-purpose flour
1 tbsp.	olive oil
3 tsp.	squid ink
5 large	eggs

For the sauce:
- Thoroughly remove the crab meat from the shells.
- In a sauce pan, heat olive oil with butter and roasted garlic. Add the crab meat and thyme, simmer for a few minutes, season with salt and pepper, then set aside.

For the leek purée:
- Slice and wash the leeks, then drain.
- In a sauce pan, brown the garlic with half of the olive oil, add the leeks, cover with a lid, and braise over a low flame until tender.
- Add the wine and cream, then purée. While puréeing, add the remaining olive oil, then season to taste.

For the pasta:
- In a bowl, beat the eggs with 1 tablespoon of oil and the squid ink; incorporate flour into eggs mixture with your fingers.
- When all ingredients are mixed thoroughly, knead dough until very elastic. Let dough rest for a while covered with plastic wrap.
- Cut the dough in small pieces and flatten them with your hand or a rolling pin. Roll pasta through a pasta machine, starting with highest setting and gradually decreasing thickness until pasta is as thin as card stock.
- Cut the pasta in squares about 1-1/2 inches wide. Then with a wooden skewer, roll each square on a ridged board starting from a corner applying enough pressure to seal pasta when roll is complete.
- Place the newly made garganello on a tray, lightly dusted with semolina flour, and cover with plastic wrap until cooking time, or freeze.
- Whether fresh or frozen, cook garganelli in abundant boiling water for a couple of minutes at most.

To complete:
- Drain and add to the crab in the sauce-pan, adding some of the cooking water at the same time. Evaporate any excess liquid.
- Spoon some leek purée into a pasta bowl. Place the pasta on top, sprinkle on some bottarga, and drizzle with extra virgin olive oil.

Wine pairing:
- Semillon Chardonnay Bin 77, Lindemans 2002

Chef Luciano Pellegrini © 2005 Valentino

Roasted Sausage-Stuffed Quails

with porcini mushrooms and polenta sformato

Serves 8

Quails

8 large	quails, deboned
8 oz.	sweet pork sausage
fresh sage	
fresh garlic to taste	
4 oz.	butter
1/2 cup	extra virgin olive oil
1 large	shallot, finely chopped
1 cup	white wine
1 cup	heavy cream
1 cup	chicken broth
1/4 cup	Italian parsley, chopped for garnish

Porcini mushrooms

1 lb.	fresh porcini (substitute 4 oz. dried if unavailable)
olive oil	
butter	
sliced garlic	

Polenta

1 cup	polenta flour
32 oz.	water
1 cup	grated parmesan cheese
1 cup	heavy cream
4 oz.	butter
fresh sage	

For the polenta:

• Bring the water to a boil, salt to taste, then pour the corn meal in, quickly beating with a whisk, and cover the pot. When the cornmeal has absorbed all the water, uncover and stir with a wooden spatula, cooking for 40 minutes on low heat.
• Bring the cream to a boil and brown the butter with some sage in a deep dish.
• Spoon in enough polenta to cover the bottom of the dish, ladle some of the cream over, sprinkle on some parmesan cheese, and douse with some brown butter. Repeat until all of the polenta is used, cover tightly, and rest in warm place for 1/2 hour.

For the porchini mushrooms:

• Clean and slice the porcini mushrooms (or soak dry ones in warm water).
• In a sauté pan, fry some sliced garlic in olive oil and a little butter. When light brown, add the porcini, season with salt and pepper, and continuously move them around with a spoon until they start exuding moisture. Cover the pan and cook over low heat for a few minutes, then set aside.

For the quail:

• Stuff the quail cavity with about 1 ounce of sausage and 1 sage leaf; close both openings with toothpicks, and brush with garlic oil.
• In a sauté pan, brown butter with a little olive oil, put the quail in, and color on all sides with the butter and garlic mixture.
• Place in an oven at 400° for 10 minutes. Remove the quail from the pan, remove toothpicks and let rest in a warm place.
• Add some chopped garlic and shallots to the pan along with some sage.
• Add the white wine and deglaze.
• When evaporated, add the cream and a little chicken broth, then simmer for a few minutes.
• Lastly, add porcini mushrooms (save some for garnish) and sprinkle abundantly with chopped parsley. Adjust seasoning.

To complete:

• Add the juices generated by the quail to the sauce.
• Place the quail in the oven for 2 more minutes.
• Spoon some of the polenta off-center onto the plate, prop the quail against it, ladle some sauce over it, and garnish with some of the porcini and fresh parsley sprigs.

Wine pairing:

• Les Lauves 2000 Jean-Luc Colombo

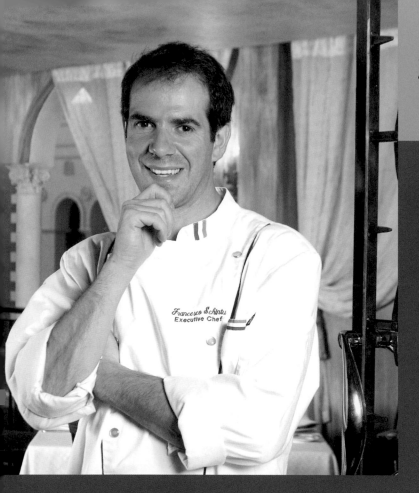

Francesco Schintu

Everything about Zeffirino says romance a la bella Italia, evoking the luxuriant Renaissance grandeur of Old World Venice. A musician strolls past your table playing an Italian love song. Gondolas on the Venetian's indoor Grand Canal glide past as you dine al fresco. Inside, the lushly decorated draped dining room is replete with an Italian-marble water well beneath a Murano glass chandelier. Art covers the soaring two-story walls and ceiling. A winding staircase leads to the main dining area that runs the length of the room with windows overlooking the canal. In a world constantly striving for the trendy and hip, this is a place to revel in tradition and elegance. Chef Francesco Schintu is right at home in such an atmosphere. "I want to give the diner the most authentic Italian experience possible," he says.

Schintu comes by his authenticity honestly: He was born in Sardinia. "I came from a poor family," he says. "My father was a farmer. My brother-in-law, Sergio, got me started in the kitchen, teaching me slowly, a few things at a time. He is a great chef and my mentor."

At 14, Schintu began an apprenticeship at the Culinary Academy of Santa Maria. It was later, during his six years as sous chef in Recco, Italy, near Genoa, that he met Gian Paulo Belloni, son of Zeffirino Belloni. Father and son had been dishing up creative Italian cuisine in their Zeffirino restaurant in Genoa since 1939, becoming a favorite of such luminaries as Frank Sinatra, Luciano Pavarotti, and Pope John Paul II.

Schintu had already made a reputation for himself and Belloni was impressed. "Many people knew me and my work," says Schintu. "Gian Paulo hired me to consult on some Italian restaurants in Quebec City, Canada."

From there it was a short journey for Schintu to take on the top job at the newly opened U. S. version of Zeffirino in Las Vegas. "Gian Paulo has given me control to do my best," says Schintu, who treats the responsibility with reverence. "I use only the best ingredients, many imported from Italy." He has his favorites: spider crab, lobster, bass, venison, rabbit, polenta, fresh pasta. "I like to mix sweet and crunchy textures with the strong flavor of the meat," Schintu says. "For example, buckwheat polenta with ricotta, or rabbit or venison with pasta. The combination of different ingredients is always amazing."

In the world of very visible celebrity chefs, Schintu is somewhat of a surprise; the dazzle of the spotlight is not for him. "I am a quiet and shy person," he confides. "I prefer the kitchen to the front of the house." He says he tries to follow his father's advice: "Always stay with your feet on the ground."

"The greatest challenge for the chef, especially here in Las Vegas, is to be himself always, and to be humble," Schintu says. "In the U.S.A., you have more opportunity to be famous, and sometimes you can forget who you are."

His ambition is to return to Italy to study at the chef school, Etoile. "This is where the champion chefs teach other very good chefs from around the world," he explains. Always striving to learn more about every area of his craft, the quiet master chef adds, "I would like to learn more about pastries."

Filet of Steak

with gnocchi and ricotta wafers

Serves 4

Steak

4 8-oz.	beef filets
1/2 cup	all-purpose flour
1/3 cup	extra virgin olive oil
1 pinch	salt
1 pinch	white pepper
1 pinch	nutmeg
10-12	Amaretto cookies ground to a powder

Marinade

3 cups	merlot or barbera wine
1 medium	shallot
2 cloves	garlic
1 medium	onion
1 sprig	rosemary
1 sprig	thyme

Sauce

2	bay leaves
1/4 cup	sugar
1/2 stick	cinnamon
1 cup	fresh blueberries

Gnocchi dough

2-3/4 cups	flour
3 whole	eggs
1 tsp.	salt
2 tbsp.	hot water
10 cups	boiling water
2 tbsp.	salt
6	sage leaves
1 tsp.	truffle oil
1/3 cup	parmesan cheese or Asiago, if available

For the marinade:
- Mix the garlic, herbs, shallot, and wine in a large bowl.
- Place the filets in the bowl and let stand for 1–3 hours.

For the sauce:
- Take the filets from the marinade and pat dry with paper towels.
- Remove herbs from the marinade and set aside.
- Put the marinade wine in a sauce pan. Add the sugar, cinnamon, and bay leaves and bring to a boil. Add blueberries and let reduce by one-third. Strain and set aside. The sauce should have a medium consistency.

For the filets:
- Heat a non-stick oven-proof sauté pan.
- Dust filets in flour. Season with salt and pepper.
- Pour olive oil in the pan; when the oil is hot, put the filets in and sear for 30 seconds per side.
- Place the pan in the oven at 375° for about 8 minutes.

For the gnocchi:
- Slowly mix the flour, salt, eggs, and water in a bowl until the dough doesn't stick.
- Wrap the ball of dough in plastic wrap and let it rest for 1/2 hour in a cool place.
- Let the dough stand at room temperature for 5 minutes.
- Cut the dough into several small pieces. Roll the dough lengthwise. Cut it into 1/2" pieces and shape into small balls.
- Place the gnocchi balls onto a tray previously dusted with flour. Set aside.

To complete the gnocchi:
- Put the gnocchi in the boiling water and salt the water (make sure it's not too salty).
- When they come to the surface, let them cook another 3 minutes.
- Drain and place in a sauté pan for a quick sauté with butter and sage.
- Place on dish and sprinkle with parmesan cheese.
- Drizzle with truffle oil.

Ricotta wafers

1 large	egg
2 tbsp.	sugar
1 tbsp.	flour
1 tsp.	saffron
1 tbsp.	port wine
1/2 cup	fresh ricotta

For the ricotta wafers:
- Mix the ricotta-wafer ingredients until smooth.
- On a baking sheet lined with parchment, make thin circles of batter about 2" in diameter.
- Bake at 325° for 15 minutes.
- Remove from oven and cool.

To complete the steak:
- Take the filet from the oven, dip one side in the reduced sauce, then dust in the cookie powder.
- Place the filet on the plate and neatly drizzle the sauce on the steak and around the plate.
- Add the gnocchi and ricotta wafers and serve.

Wine pairing:
- Borolo Nearvasco Bersano 1996

GLOSSARY

Brunoise: A fine dice measuring 1/4 inch square.

Cèpe: A pale-brown mushroom with a smooth meaty texture; also known as Porcini.

Chinoise: A cone-shaped very fine meshed strainer.

Confit: Usually meat such as goose, duck, or pork slowly cooked in its own fat. Garlic can also be cooked this way.

Croustillant: An outside wrap, fried for a crispy finish.

Demi-glace: A rich brown sauce of reduced veal stock.

Deglaze: To add a small amount of wine or stock to a pan after browning meat, removing the meat from the pan, and discarding excess grease in order to make a base for a sauce.

Feuille de Brick: A French term for a sheet of flaky pastry; puff pastry.

French: To cut meat and fat away from the end of a rib or chop, leaving the bones bare.

Frisse: A curly slender-leafed lettuce of the chicory family.

Ganache: A rich chocolate mixture of semi-sweet chocolate and whipping cream.

Garganelli: A quill-shaped pasta.

Glace: Also Glace de Viande, veal stock reduced to a syrupy consistency and intense flavor.

Haricot verts: Very thin young green beans.

Julienne: Foods that have been cut into thin matchstick strips.

Jus: French for juice or a thin gravy.

Irish Mist: A liquor made from a blend of Irish whiskey and heather honey.

Lardons: Bacon that has been diced, blanched in water, and fried until brown.

Mandoline: A rectangular food slicer with interchangeable blades that vary the thickness, shape, and design of the slices.

Micro greens: Immature very small greens.

Mirin: A low-alcohol, sweet, golden wine made from glutinous rice.

Pancetta: Italian bacon cured with salt and spices, but not smoked.

Pancetta lardon: A large slice of pork fat back, cured in salt; lardon is the fat flavorings remaining when the pancetta is cooked with other ingredients and used for seasoning in the recipe.

Panko: Coarse bread crumbs used in Japanese cooking for coating fried foods.

Pappadam: A very thin wafer-like bread from India made from lentils.

Polenta bramata: High-quality flour made from stone-ground grains of corn and buckwheat.

Poussin: A very young, small chicken.

Raita: Yogurt salads made of whole-milk yogurt and chopped fruit or vegetables and seasoned with black mustard sees and herbs. Designed as a cooling counterbalance for many spicy Indian dishes.

Reduce: To boil a liquid (usually stock, wine, or a sauce mixture) rapidly until the volume is reduced by evaporation, thereby thickening the consistency and intensifying the flavor.

Roux: A mixture of equal amounts flour and butter used to thicken sauces and soups.

Sea Boat scallops: Very large wild scallops.

Season to taste: To add salt and fresh ground pepper to your preference.

Silpat mat: A non-stick baking sheet that transfers heat to the food without burning.

Stock: The strained liquid from cooked vegetables, meat bones or fish bones, water, and herbs.

Sweat: To cook in a small amount of fat over low heat. The ingredients are covered with a piece of foil or parchment paper, then the pot is tightly covered. The ingredients soften without browning and cook in their own juices.

Tourne: To trim vegetables into a uniform seven sided football shape.

Sources:
"The Food Lover's Companion" by Sharon Tyler Herbst
"The New Larousse Gastronomique" by Prosper Montagne

159

RECIPE CHALLENGE INDEX

The following list delineates the challenge, on a scale of 1 to 5, of preparing the recipes of Las Vegas celebrity chefs. They're listed in order of difficulty—from least difficult (1) to most difficult (5)—within their particular food categories.

FINDING A MATE

Pairing the Right Wine with the Right Food

Fine food deserves fine wine. But gone are the days of the stuffy old canon that decreed white wine for fish and red for meat. "I always say, drink what you like," states Alpana Singh, 28, the youngest woman Master Sommelier in the U.S. and head of the wine cellar at Jean Joho's Everest restaurant in Chicago.

These days, pairing wine and food hinges on the taste you're seeking, giving consideration to the ingredients of the food, the spices used, and how the food is cooked. The key to success is to balance the weight of the food with the weight of the wine, regardless of the color of either. Chicken for example. "Is it a baked chicken?" asks Singh. "Baking is considered a delicate more elegant preparation, so you might pair a light wine with it. But if the chicken is barbecued, which has a more rugged bolder flavor, then perhaps a more hearty aromatic wine is in order."

Wine can also complement or contrast with the flavor of your meal. For example, Singh suggests that if the food is fried, the crunchy oiliness of the fat can be cut with a highly acidic wine. "For example, salmon is a very oily fish," she says. "That makes a Pinot Noir a classic pairing."

Choosing a wine should be fun, not intimidating or overwhelming. "Most sommeliers, my peers, are anxious to break down the mystique and introduce the world of wine to everyone, no matter what level of wine drinker he or she might be," asserts Singh. "There is no right or wrong in enjoying any wine with good food."

Ordering an expensive wine is no longer associated with sophistication, insists Singh. "Price is no longer the significant factor in wine selection. Experience is," she says.

"Ordering an expensive wine isn't a satisfying experience if the person ordering doesn't feel comfortable or like the taste."

In today's global economy, with increased international travel, people are discovering wonderful new wine offerings. "Once you have tried a particular brand, style, or country, you are more open to try other versions of the same," suggests Singh. "This is an educational process. The enjoyment in wine tasting is as much the ambience of the experience as it is the knowledge gained when learning about the history of the region, the vineyard, the grapes, and the process."

According to *Wine Spectator's* "Guide to Great Wine Values," wines flow from lightest to heaviest in this order: Soave, Orvieto, Pinot Grigio, Riesling, Muscadet, Champagne, Chenin Blanc, French Chablis, Sauvignon Blanc, white Bordeaux, white Burgundy, Pinot Gris (Alsace, Tokay), Gewürztraminer, United States or Australia Chardonnay, Valpolicella, Beaujolais, Dolcetto, Rioja, California Pinot Noir, Burgundy, Barbera, Chianti Classico, Barbaresco, Barolo, Bordeaux, Merlot, Zinfandel, Cabernet Sauvignon, Rhône, Syrah, Shiraz.

The locations of the vineyards that produce these offerings are as diverse as the grapes themselves. Chili, Bulgaria, Brazil, and New Zealand produce excellent-quality table wines, expanding the selections once controlled by France and Italy. California, Spain, Austria, Greece, and Australia bring even more diversity to the table.

So go ahead, start sipping. If you like what you taste, and you like the way it matches your food, then you've chosen the perfect wine for your meal.